W. JONES LOFLIN

PRIME RIB
OR
POTTED MEAT?

Thoughts on Getting
More Out of Life

PRIME RIB OR POTTED MEAT?
Thoughts on Getting More Out of Life

Jones Loflin

Copyright 1998

Library of Congress Catalog Card Number: 97-095314
ISBN #: 0-9662361-0-6

Publisher:

H.O.P.E. Inc. Press
118 East Lawyers Road
Monroe, NC 28110
(704) 753-4811

Additional copies of *PRIME RIB OR POTTED MEAT?* may be obtained from the publisher.

Cover design and book layout by Lisa B. Loflin

To my wonderful wife, Lisa, and perfect daughter, Alex. Your presence in my life is a constant reminder of the value in living a life of prime rib instead of potted meat.

Acknowledgments

To my parents, whose nurturing and unconditional love gave me the desire to pursue the best ideals in life. Your deep spiritual faith and concern for the well-being of others are a constant living example for me and were the key inspirations for writing this book.

To my wife, Lisa, the greatest spouse in the world. Thank you for believing in me even when I didn't believe in myself, and for your patience with my impatience when putting this book together. Your design of the cover and layout of the book is perfect. I have no idea how I will repay you for all the days you spent getting everything just right.

To my daughter, Alex. Thank you for reminding me that each moment of our lives is precious, and that the simple pleasures in life are the best ones.

To Bob and Carol Saks, Bob and Sharon Zinser, and Angelene Keziah for your proofreading of the chapters. Your support and wisdom are appreciated more than you will ever know.

To Jack Gale, an extraordinary man. Your painstakingly thorough editing of the manuscript was incredible. Your knowledge of the English language and grasp of proper writing styles was invaluable in the completion of this project. Thank You!

To Patrick Grady-a marvelous mentor. The long phone conversations and business discussions are a breath of fresh air in such a challenging career. Most importantly, thanks for your friendship.

To all the relatives, friends, acquaintances, and even strangers who were the inspiration for many of the stories in this book.

Lastly, to all those people whose prime-rib lives have been a blueprint for my own journey. May this book reflect positively upon your presence in my life.

The Menu

Reading The Menu

Growing up in a rural area of North Carolina was one of the greatest things that ever happened to me. I was instilled with those small town values so many people desperately desire for their own children today. I went to a relatively small school (76 in my graduating class) where each teacher knew not only their students, but most of the other students in the building as well. My mom was home in the evenings and my dad was, too. The vast majority of the community knew the young people in their town and were quick to point out to our parents any mischief in which we were involved.

My experiences in Davidson County also taught me to enjoy the simple pleasures in life. Swimming in freshwater lakes, fishing in private ponds, and hunting in beautiful wooded areas around the county. Attending local sporting events, evenings with relatives, and active participation in a church were also a staple of living there.

The most unique aspect of growing up in this area, however, was my exposure to exotic foods. No, I do not mean caviar or Filet Mignon or baked Alaska. I am referring to fried okra, country ham, rabbit, deer (venison for those who are above their raising) and squirrel. Turtle soup was also a stop on my culinary adventure. By far the most unique delicacy to cross my lips, however, was potted meat.

Since some of you will be opening this book after a meal, I will dispense with the intimate details of the ingredients of this mushy delight. Suffice it to say that potted meat is the conglomeration of many things left over from the processing of swine. These parts, not good for anything else, are thrown together, ground and blended to a smooth consistency and then loaded with a huge amount of spices and flavorings to make it more palatable. Its high amount of salt is one of its endearing qualities since it will keep forever without spoiling.

My father got a great sense of satisfaction from having me try certain foods like potted meat. At lunch time we would try not only potted meat, but also sardines, Vienna sausages, and liver pudding (not at the same meal, however). Although I did develop a taste for sardines for a while, the other items never seemed to catch on in my "Most Favorite Foods" category. The memories, however, are priceless.

At the other end of the food chain is prime rib. Several years ago while in college I was travelling as a national officer of a youth organization. While in the Midwest one evening, I saw a sign that read, "Prime Rib....All You Can Eat." I will refrain from telling you the cost since it would date me. Securing the approval of the individual with me, we guided the automobile into the restaurant parking lot. It was a cold winter evening, and the table next to the fireplace was perfect. Soon, the platter of marvelous meat and potato arrived. Taking my first bite, I was in my own little world. I even remarked to one group that it tasted so good I hated to swallow it. Needless to say, I did swallow that bite and many others. It was a wonderful evening.

For those of you agriculturally challenged, prime rib is one of the most valuable parts of beef cattle. Well, next to the hide used for those tennis shoes on which you have to make payments. In Japan, there is a region within the country where livestock farmers actually massage the animal to make the prime rib even more tender. Imagine that in *your* local community the next time you see a field of cattle. You would definitely respond, "Yes, I do believe Farmer John's butter has slipped off his biscuit" (i.e. lost his mind).

It is my belief that people reflect prime rib or potted meat tendencies in their own lives. Potted meat people rarely attempt to get the best out of life, instead choosing to throw together all the responsibilities of their life with their talent and energy. They grind them up with the frantic rush of living for the moment and season it with frustration, disappointment, and an occasional achievement made in spite of their haphazard approach. Their lives, like a can of potted meat, hold little value to them, causing them an even greater sense of futility.

Prime rib people, on the other hand, are constantly looking for the best things in life. They search for ways to improve their relationships, sharpen their career skills, and help other people make life more meaningful. They are typically patient, knowing that their ideal life will not quickly come to pass, but will require a massaging of sort, working through every aspect of their lives, making changes and improvements as necessary. The result is not always measured in terms of financial gain or great power, but in the satisfaction that life has been lived to its fullest, with little remorse about missed opportunities or lost relationships. Like my meal by the fireplace, prime rib people want other people to enjoy all life has to offer as well.

This book is a conglomeration of many elements which I believe would create a prime rib life. I say "many," because there are obviously more to be discussed by me or someone else in another day. Frequently reflecting on my own life while writing this book, I became keenly aware of some areas in my own life which could use some serious improvement.

As you begin reading the book, I encourage you to scan the table of contents to find the chapters that most interest you at this stage in your life. Reading these first will prevent you from filling up on an appetizer before you get to the main course. Having met your mental dietary needs, sample the other chapters to perhaps gain a new appreciation for some entrees you have tried before or ones never experienced. For example, you might have never read any books on money management. Reading that chapter, however, may spur you on to delving into a similar topic more intensely later. For your dessert, may I suggest the zeal chapter, which is a satisfying culmination of what I trust will be a great dining experience.

As you finish the book, I sincerely hope you find yourself coming back again and again, to try old favorites or experience the joy of a chapter passed over a previous time. Invite your friends to try the book, with the expectation that it will help them in their quest to be prime rib people as well.

A

Ability

Your abilities.... For as long as I can remember, I have always heard, "Find something you are good at and find a career to match it." I am still in search of a career that will allow me to read *Calvin and Hobbes* cartoons, eat steak and cheesecake, and take afternoon naps. In an ideal world, the concept is seemingly a good one. However, it does not take two important factors into account:

Developed skills and abilities

Since most of us are not a child prodigy or genius, we have, over time, been introduced to a variety of tasks requiring a huge array of skills for their completion. It is these experiences that have introduced us to things we do and do not find appealing. The problem arises when many people stop looking for those experiences to further explore their abilities.

During my first year of teaching (the year I thought I knew everything), I taught vocational education, which means that I instructed students on general job skills that would fit them for a variety of occupations. One of my favorite subjects to teach was woodworking. Once introduced to the safe and proper use of shop equipment, students were required to build a project.

Joey was one of my students who thought he had learned enough by the time he was in the ninth grade to be successful in life. Each day as we began the demonstrations of shop equipment, Joey would reply that he had never used that item before and did not know how to operate it. I tried to illustrate to him that the reason he was in school was to learn new skills that could prepare him for life. Joey's comment: "I'll just use another tool I know how to use." Another student, Brandon, was also unsure of the use of shop equipment but asked frequent questions throughout the process. Visiting Brandon a few months later, I was surprised to see a band saw in his car port. When I asked him about, it he said, "I really enjoyed using one in your class, and my parents bought one for me." Brandon had accepted the challenge education brings and grown in his skills because of it. Many people, young and old, are like Joey. They deny themselves the illuminating opportunity to discover new skill interests because they do not want to step out of their comfort zone.

Fear of failure limits our skill development

"It is better to have tried and failed than not to have tried at all" is another over-used phrase in our society. It might more appropriately be stated, "It is better to have tried, failed and learned from it than not to have tried at all." Too often, we may try and fail and leave it there. We do not mentally consider failure a learning process but instead let it deflate our self-esteem, reducing our expectations for the next venture.

I always wanted to be an athlete. Now those of you who have seen me in person are laughing hysterically. My height is 5'7" and weight is around 180 (depending on how much I can lean on the scale and distort the readings). Throughout my school years I have been 20-30 pounds overweight, quite a stumbling block toward an athletic career.

That did not stop me, however. Since second grade I have tried out for everything from tee ball to football to basketball. In tee ball they took everybody, so I was on a team. While in junior high I tried out for football and went home scared to death. When my dad inquired about the look of terror in my face, I said, "We were told to run laps around the football field, and after the first lap I could not catch my breath." Oh well, so much for my hope of sympathy. My dad laughed and replied, "Son, you are out of shape. Run some everyday and those pains will go away." Me, run? Everyday!? How about once a month? I quit football tryouts the next day.

My final attempt at athletics was during my freshman year in high school. Junior Varsity basketball. My chance of making it were quite good that year since the entire high school only had 325 students. Those who were competent with dribbling and shooting a basketball were on varsity....perhaps this would be the end to almost a decade of failure. Tryouts were held for 3 days, and the coach announced on Friday night that the players making the team would be listed on his classroom door Monday. I could not sleep all weekend just thinking about how I would finally get to wear a uniform and be part of an athletic team because I had earned it.

Monday arrived. I hurried down the wood-floored hall, hoping to be the first to read the list. Some students had already arrived and were looking at the list. Straining with my eyes I saw....Gary, Dennis, Skipper...but not Jones. Turning and walking up the hall, I could have just crawled under a rock. My big chance....gone.

Walking toward my first period class, a voice behind me said, "Hey Jones, I need to talk with you!" It was our athletic director. He said, "I see you didn't make the basketball team." At this point slugging him became a very viable option. Instead, I merely lowered my head and replied, "Yep, same old story." His comment in return shocked me. He said, "We are in need of an announcer for our varsity basketball teams. In talking with several teachers, they suggested you. You have an interest in athletics and seem to have a gift for speaking."

My first thought was to say, "Nice try on cheering me up." Instead, I pondered the opportunity and agreed to accept it on a trial basis. My first season was hideous. I mispronounced opposing players' names (which almost got me in several fights with irate parents) and often credited the wrong player with a foul or basket. I made it, however, and things improved over the next year. Soon I was announcing varsity football and a variety of other school activities (I once even commentated on a ping pong tournament.. that will tell you about the level of excitement in our high school).

To bring an end to a very long story, that opportunity came as a result of not being afraid of failing. Those early days of speaking to audiences were a rung in the ladder of preparation for my career as a professional speaker. I would never have had that opportunity if I had not been attempting to achieve the goal of making a sports team. As it turned out, I not only became a part of several sports teams but got some early training for my career.

Choosing a career that matches your skills does not guarantee satisfaction

College was a tremendous learning experience for me (the classes were kind of fun, too). In the fall semester of my freshman year I took Animal Science (my major was agricultural education). As we loaded the bus for our first animal science lab, visions of grandeur danced in my head. Would we be looking at gene splicing? Perhaps we would witness some other cutting edge technology that would revolutionize the animal science industry.

We unloaded the bus at a somewhat normal-looking barn. The professor stepped in front of the group and announced, "Today we will be palpating the testicles of rams." For those of you who do not have an animal husbandry background that meant that we were going to check for tumors in the reproductive organs of male sheep. Talk about disappointment. What a ridiculous activity for such enlightened minds. I knew better than to plead my case, however, and began the mundane activity. One would hold the ram while the other would....well, you have the picture by now.

While performing this somewhat unnatural assignment, I happened to notice a girl close by working with her ram. Her face was wrinkled like she had eaten a green persimmon (something very puckery for those of you who are persimmon deprived), and she seemed to be in agony. It was also during this time that I noted that she was rather attractive. Upon completion of our lab, I made sure to sit next to this exquisite lady. We began a conversation and made small talk for a few moments. I asked her about her major, and she proudly announced, "Pre-vet. I want to become a veterinarian. I just love being around animals." Her answer immediately assured me that this young maiden did not have the intelligence to be the future Ms. Loflin.

Now, I realize that while in college she could have overcome her fear of working with animals (exhibited by her displeasure in working with the sheep), but I somehow sensed that a career as a veterinarian would not be all she planned for it to be. For one thing, you must keep both eyes open when performing surgery on any animal. How many individuals find a career that seemingly matches their abilities, only to find after one month, one week or one year that something has gone greatly amiss? What happened? They failed to look at the big picture....seeing the entire career with all its responsibilities and daily routine instead of just what obvious skills were needed.

A More Effective Process

Whether you are 12 or 72, there are ways to make solid career choices with your abilities as the focal point. The key is to genuinely ask yourself these questions:

1) What do I want to do with my life? Answering this question before choosing a career path or before modifying one can make a tremendous difference. Answering this question in the context of career development or change will bring to the surface the rewards of your occupation and your impact on your family, friends and your community. Too many times we settle into a "temporary" career while waiting for something else to come along or when financial needs demand it. Unfortunately, we often stay in that career for years and years, expending our resources of time and mental and physical energy, never growing ourselves toward those lofty ambitions we once had. More specifically, ask yourself:

- What values do I live by that I want exemplified in my career?
- What type of lifestyle must be supported by the income from this career?
- What kind of work schedule am I attempting to find?
- How many years do I want to work? Will I be physically able to meet the demands of this job in 10, 20 or 30 years?

2) Am I willing to make sacrifices to get to my more desirable career? An honest answer to such a question as this will immediately put things into perspective. A high school student probably would have very little to sacrifice (besides being away from family and a high school "sweetie") if they made the decision to go to college or join the military, whereas someone in their forties would have a spouse, mortgage and children to think about before they upgraded their career skills or took a job that would require new training and a reduction in income.

Teachers are a perfect case study when understanding peoples' unwillingness to sacrifice. Having been a teacher in different schools, I have listened to a multitude of teachers air their grievances about being a part of the education process. The statement that will ultimately come from their mouth is, "I am going to find something else to do." Upon further inquiry, I would hear visions of getting involved in sales or marketing, running their own business, or other outstanding career choices. In my naive days I would ask, "Then why don't you go after it?" Their response was typically that in two more years they would be in a better position because of the age of their children or they would be more financially stable later. These appeared to be valid reasons but were really only surface ones.

It was my financial planner who assisted in bringing to the surface the *real* reasons why those disgruntled teachers would not make a career move. In conversations similar to the ones I had with discontent teachers, he would ask, "Are you willing to work five days a week until six or seven o'clock for the first couple years?" "Oh no," came the teacher's reply, "I like being home most days by 4:30." Continuing to dig, he would inquire, "Are you willing to take a pay cut for a year or two while you gain experience and learn the ropes of a business or organization?" The teacher's response: "Oh no, I have to make at least x number of dollars each year. I could not make any less." By then my thoughts were like the doctor performing surgery-I think we have struck a nerve.

Please understand that I am not making light of a person's financial or personal obligations. Moreover, I am not singling out just teachers. I hear it from all walks of life, but my background is in education. It just seems that many people expect to leave a job with ten to twenty years of experience and walk into another career and get paid the same or better immediately. If there were no sacrifices to be made to get to the other career, everyone would already be there!

My wife, Lisa, and I were blessed to have been taught very sound money management principles both by our parents and by several trusted friends early in our marriage. So when we began our dream (a business in public speaking), the sacrifices were not as scary as one might think. In the first two years we did live on just one income while income from public speaking was returned to the business as operating capital. That meant less money for all areas of our life. We knew, however, that what we gave up in monetary compensation those early years would be gained in time together as a family and development of a business that would have untold rewards in the years to come.

One of my favorite "non-sacrifice" stories deals with a librarian. Soon after I left my last teaching position, Mr. Librarian (names have been changed to protect the embarrassed) stopped by my house to inquire about my plans. With a wisp of fear in my voice, I told him of my long range plan of becoming a professional public speaker. He mulled it over for a moment and then remarked, "You know, I always wanted to try something like that." He then embarked upon an elaborate idea about talking with different groups and some rewarding experiences he had had in public speaking. We finished our conversation and he drove away. As I walked back to the house, I was confused beyond my normal levels. Let us compare Mr. Librarian's situation with mine. I am 28, married, and have a 25-year mortgage on my home. Mr. Librarian is 60 something, unmarried, and lives in a beautiful home where he grew up. He has accumulated wealth untold over the years from an inheritance and a steady income from education. Now you tell me, am I missing something here? Shouldn't *I* be the one going to Mr. Librarian's house to tell *him* of my dream of success? Why didn't he venture out years ago. The worst case scenario would put him back in education after a two or three year absence, with more new experiences to share with students and others. The difference was Mr. Librarian was not willing to sacrifice. Perhaps things are not quite as simple for your situation, but I would be willing to bet that there are some sacrifices that could begin moving you in the direction of your ideal career.

3) Are you willing to swallow your shallow pride? This question is largely directed toward any males who are reading this book. Changing careers and/or preparing for a new direction in life often requires a level of humility not found in the psyche of many of us. Men are conquerors (see XY chapter) and often do not like having to be conquered for even a short time.

In my senior year at college Lisa and I began the process of on-campus interviews for possible teaching positions. Our education area was fairly specialized (Agriculture Education), so getting a job did not appear to be easy. During our interviews, however, we began to see that administrators who were looking for agricultural education teachers liked what they saw in us. That is not bragging but rather a credit to all the individuals who had saw fit to make us what we are. Getting a job proved to be easier than we thought. We felt a great sense of pride because others saw value in us.

Enter a reality check. My first six months of full-time public speaking were a challenge to say the least. Even with securing contacts, developing address lists, and mailing promotional packets, I had two or three days a week that I could spend on something else. To supplement our income I did everything from substitute teaching to clerical work to minor desktop publishing. The difficult part would come when someone saw me at a place of part-time work and comment, "I thought you were going to be a professional speaker. What are you doing here?" No matter what my response, their reaction, spoken or unspoken, was usually, "Oh, so maybe things aren't so easy." Their glares and comments hurt more as I thought about the faith my wife and parents had in me and how they must be facing a similar kind of ridicule.

For most males it is tough to appear unsuccessful in a career choice we *choose* to make. We do not have the luxury of being down on our luck or a victim of circumstance. We cannot even use the crutch of downsizing or medical conditions. This uncomfortable situation has been brought to light several times in an activity called "Insights." In this activity, participants sit in a circle and are asked a question. Each person must then respond with their answer. No one is exempt from responding to the question. One of the questions presented to the group is, "What one thing makes you most secure?" Men in the group have frequently responded that their career or job was one main source of security. Think about your own life. When we meet others, one of the first questions we ask is, "What do you do for a living?" If we are currently unsure of success in our career choice, this question becomes a type of emotional sword that cuts to the heart of our very being.

What I find ironic about this pride problem is that, in the true sense of conquerors, people should actually take more pride in the fact that they are attempting to conquer the dragons of uncertainty and failure instead of wimping out by staying in their comfort zone. As Thoreau said, "Most people live lives of quiet desperation." Thank goodness for the ones who are not quiet about their desperate desire to make more of their lives and attempt those things that might lead to failure but might also lead to new inventions, ideas, or concepts that go far beyond individual success. As one bumper sticker read, "Those who abandon their dreams will discourage yours." Watch out for those individuals who attempt to take your true pride away by belittling your dreams and aspirations. Often they are simply envious that you had the intestinal fortitude to seek more out of life.

4) Do you have the relationships to support your plans or change of plans, etc.? With everything else in order (correct answers to questions 1-3), the answer "No" to this question can stop you dead in your tracks. Yes, there are countless stories of people who have achieved their goals in spite of little or no support from family and friends. My response to that statement is, "Yes, but it was probably a much more difficult process because of a lack of support from others." As individuals we have the greatest ingredient for success right in front of us, but overlook its value. Our relationships with others can be the fuel that keeps us going when we have exhausted our own energy. Their belief in us keeps us afloat when we are drowning in doubt or failure. What I am not talking about is "networking" types of relationships. Numerous books and courses develop those skills. I am talking about emotional relationships that transcend career success or failure. Let's look at a house as an example.

When you build a house, you start with footings and a foundation capable of supporting the structure above it. The building materials, floor plan, and house trim can change dramatically *as long as* the proper foundation is in place. Your relationships with your family and friends are like the footings and foundations. As long as those are in order, you can, within a great range, pursue myriad career options within your lifetime. Why? Because those individuals are not supporting you for your similarity to their business interests but rather are supporting you because of what you are in their life - Roles like a parent, spouse, child or community member. These roles include deep emotional bonds that tend to stay intact regardless of occupational choice or success in that career choice. Networking relationships, as described in business, are like suppliers of the material you may use to build your house (i.e. brick, wood) or architects who specialize in a specific area of construction. If you change the type of materials or layout of the home (careers), you may need to change suppliers or architects (network). We need consistency in such a tumultuous world.

Summing It Up

Starting with your abilities in mind is not always the best way to determine your future career path or career change. Looking at the big picture, which includes the impact you want to make on society and the quantity/quality time you want to spend with your family and friends, plays a major role in determining the use of those abilities.

Once you choose a career direction, you must be willing to sacrifice in the short term to get to your long-term goals. Be aware of the perils of career changes, perils that include increased humility, uncomfortable speculation from others, and a need for strong relationships to make it through the tough times.

Above all else, remember, "As the want gets stronger, the how gets easier."

B

Building Bridges

A common phrase often shared with me is "I could never talk with people the way you do." As I travel across the country, I get into numerous conversations with people in airports, hotels, and restaurants. We talk about all the usual stuff like my accent (perhaps you remember my phrase, "I don't have an accent....you do"), North Carolina culture, and my two last names. (I actually have three last names-my first name is Wiley. Strangely enough, I married a girl with three first names, Lisa Yvette Bryan). Once the small talk is out of the way, I hear some form of the statement, "I could never talk with people the way you do." What they mean is that they are just not comfortable talking with people they do not know. My first reaction is to say, "And you think I am?" But I realize that might not bode well for my professional nature, so I say, "Don't be so hard on yourself, it is not as difficult as it seems." With my professional integrity now intact, we continue talking about other things.

Let me fill you in on a little secret: The most difficult part about being a speaker is communicating quickly with a group of strangers. As much as I love being around people, the greatest source of anxiety for me has always been getting in the midst of a group of people I have never met and somehow moving beyond small talk. My fear is not that people will say, "Oh, that Jones Loflin is such a great guy," but instead that I will not be able to express who I am through my words with them. From my beginnings as a chapter officer in a high school organization to my days as a teacher to today, I have come to realize that it is the one-on-one conversations with people that often make the most impact on them. Eloquent words shared on stage can be quickly forgotten if I am unable to communicate with people on a more personal level after the program is over.

The business world has wrestled with the problem of improving interpersonal communications for years. Check out the business section at any bookstore, and you will see countless books and audio-video materials on getting the customer to say yes. You can also enroll in any number of self-help seminars that will teach you an intense process to use to get positive results from your potential clients. Salespeople who have a proven track record seem to have a "knack" for talking with people, and their underlings often attempt to imitate their process with little or no success.

Ironically, we have used an effective system for years to communicate with others. We have used it so much, in fact, that it has become a passive process instead of an active one. In this chapter we will look at one plan for helping you build a bridge to others that can carry your thoughts clearly to them and vice versa. What's more, it can be used by anyone from a three-year-old to a corporate executive. It works whether you are trying to get someone to join a civic club or consider buying a product or service. It's a process so simple, even a UNC graduate could understand it. (Perhaps you ought to know that UNC stands for the University of North Carolina, the arch rival of my alma mater, NC State University.). It is called the ABC technique.

ABC Technique
>   A   **Ask Questions**
>   B   **Build Bridges**
>   C   **Capture Commitment**

A   Ask Questions

Sound simple? Asking questions *is* simple. The difficult part is asking the *right* questions. Need a quick example? Consider the telemarketer, a master in this process. You pick up the phone and a voice says, "Hi, may I speak with _____." If you match their name request and choose not to hang up on them (as many of us do) they will quickly fire off a question like, "Would you like to save 25% on your long distance?" or "Do you have a home with gutters?" or "Do you have a computer in your home?" They know how to bypass the small talk and immediately grab your attention. (I have to admit, incidentally, that in my disdain for such overly ambitious phone mongers, I have begun to give sarcastic responses to their questions. If they ask about saving money on long distance, I tell them, "No, I like paying higher rates" or "what is a computer" if they inquire about one.)

In relationships with people, the goal is not to make them arrogant toward us but to create an environment of interest in us and/or our product or service. When you meet people for the first time, begin with the obvious small talk questions but quickly move to questions that hone in on an area that will be helpful as you begin explaining your product, service, or organization. Let's look at some situations.

Situation One. One of the most dreaded parts of your job is to attend an annual trade show and represent your company. Your duties include standing in a booth and talking with prospective customers about your company's products. After the first few hours you are ready to crawl under a rock. It seems like every person you make eye contact with just veers away from your area. You check your breath, make sure there is no food on your face, and try to figure out why people are not flocking to your booth. Instead of planning a career change (see ability chapter), you begin the ABC technique. You check people's clothing for signs of a company name, home state, or other point of conversation (lapel pins, buttons, stickers, monogrammed emblems, tote bags, etc.) You ask them questions about the item(s) and find out from one attendee that they are from Utah. You heart jumps a beat because Utah is in your sales territory.

Situation Two. As a member of a local civic organization, you are interested in getting a local business owner to consider joining your group. You have two ways to handle this situation. One is to make small talk and then come right out with the question: "John, we would love to have you join our organization." From John's angle, you have just asked him to add one more thing to his already busy schedule. His likely response will be, "I'll think about it."

Our alternative approach works like this. You notice that John really seems to enjoy helping his customers. You also notice a plaque of appreciation from a local recreational league. You now begin the ABC technique by asking John about the plaque and how he got it. His reply is that he sponsored a tee ball team. A large smile fills his face as he talks fondly about how cute all those seven and eight year olds were running around the field.

The common denominator in both these scenarios is that you took the focus off yourself and shifted it to the other person. When you ask questions, the other person becomes interested because you are showing an initial interest in who *they* are. You no longer have the immediate pressure of proving yourself or the worth of your product or service. Remember, the goal in this entire process is to create an environment of shared information, not a win-lose proposition. The key is to ask those types of questions that lead to things the other person has in common with your product, service, or organization. That is where Part B kicks into the picture.

B   Build Bridges

Returning to our stressed-out trade show representative, we find him now saying to the prospective client, "A minute ago you mentioned you're from Utah. We have several distribution centers in Utah. What part of Utah are you from?" Now, class, you are catching on at this point. By asking the right questions, this employee has a clear direction to take this conversation. He is quickly approaching Part C.

Meanwhile, back at John's store, the civic club member responds to John's comments about the tee ball team. He says, "That is great, John! Our civic club sponsors Operation Santa Claus, which provides clothing and toys to needy children in the community." Plucking at his heart strings, you say? Okay, maybe, but remember the goal-to get John to say yes to joining the civic club. Instead of saying no because John sees the club just as something else to do, John now has a clearer picture of the club and one of its purposes. His interest has just met your club's interest on the bridge we have built.

Still not convinced? Go back to our tenacious telemarketer. After the question about saving on long distance and our positive correct response, they will reply with, "Great, we thought you might. _____ (long distance company) has a plan that can save you up to 25% on your long distance calls." Once common interests have been established, people are much more willing to listen to our information.

C   Capture Commitment

Business courses call this closing the sale. Once we have built the bridge between us and the other person, we must get them to agree, or, in some form, to cross it. Hence, capturing a commitment.

Returning to our trade show, the company representative says, "I have enjoyed talking with you, Joe. Before you go, can I get your address? I'd like to send you some product information." Granted, the business gurus have a million better questions than that, but the concept is sound. We must get some type of commitment from the other person at the time the bridge is built. If we wait until later to ask for commitment, the bridge may have been eroded by time or a change in circumstances. Getting a commitment now insures that we can continue the building process in the future without having to start at "A" again.

Realizing your time with John in his store is quickly dwindling, you ask him to come to your next club meeting or to be your guest at a club outing. His response has a much greater chance of being "Yes" because he sees a bridge between his interests and those of the organization.

Several years ago I was an officer of a national youth organization. A portion of my duties included attending state conferences and meeting with members of the organization. As I said earlier, I enjoy being with people, but it was with a great deal of apprehension that I attended my first state conference. It was in Massachusetts. Read on.

In case you have forgotten, I am from North Carolina. The cultural differences between the two states was enough to create an awkward situation. Being my little naive self, however, I arrived at the registration area, prepared to mingle and get to know the members. After about ten minutes, I was ready to go home. I walked around, hoping to be invited to join in the conversation as I would back in the South, but it did not work. People would just glance at me and then continue on with their stuff. I have never taken rejection with good grace (although the girls of my dating years gave me a vast experience with the concept), so my solution was obvious: I returned to my hotel room to pout.

As I sat in my room, all I could think about was, "What can I talk to them about? What can I say that will make them talk to me. What is it that people like to talk about? Of course... they like to talk about themselves!" My wife says that I am not always the sharpest pencil in the drawer. Armed with this new-found wisdom, I returned to the registration area. One bus had driven up and, as the students filed off with their luggage, one student had a suitcase covered in stickers. I asked about the stickers and found out she was a member of a band that had performed all across the country. Soon I saw a student who had a Duke University hat. Asking about it, I found out they had a brother attending that university. Since Duke University is in North Carolina, we struck up a conversation about their perception of North Carolina. All this may seem trivial to you, but the relief to me was incredible. Asking questions of the other person opened the door to honest, deeper conversations about life and their interests. Finally, we could take the information gained in our conversation and make commitments (either spoken or unspoken) to improve our lives, even if we just had a better appreciation of the value of others.

A Final Thought

The ABC technique is a simple procedure to use when our goal is a meaningful, goal-oriented conversation that builds a bridge of relationship instead of just exchanging small talk. It does require effort on our part to ask the right questions and to be a good listener (See jabber chapter). Even my two-and-a-half-year-old daughter knows how to use the process, and I have never taught it to her (perhaps she has read my notes). When she wants one of her favorite foods (i.e. cookies, candy or a Yoo Hoo [chocolate drink]) she will come to me and say, "Daddy, you hungry?" (Asking Question) Following my positive response, it's "Me hungry, too" (Building Bridges), followed by "You want to get some candy?" (Capture Commitment) My response?... must you even ask?

C

Character

The word "character" is rarely used in today's society other than to describe someone who is witty or lively. Oh, and it may be used when describing an animated or cartoon individual. Its lack of use to me seemingly highlights a flaw in our being. We have become so caught up in achieving materialistic goals that we have forgotten that *who* we are is more important than *what* we are or what positions we achieve in our professional careers. How did we get to this point? What is the underlying cause? Here is my prognosis.

Person vs. Performance

Years ago (long before I was born), before the age of mobile or transplanted families, our character was of great importance. People generally lived in communities where they knew a large number of other people, and they created an environment in which people relied on other people for their support and possible career advancement. If John or Joann went to the local bank to apply for a job, the bank president would probably know their parents and have some knowledge of John or Joann's background. These two bright young kids knew that they better keep their "nose" clean if they wanted to get that first job.

Additionally, most of the other members of the community watched their P's and Q's as well because they knew if they messed up, everyone in the community would soon find out about it.

Another facet of that time was church attendance. Now hang on, I am not implying that all church members were people of impeccable character. Just think about the accountability, however. If you were a member of a church, you had a group of people who saw you almost every week, and if you weren't there, they would often check up on you. If nothing else, you felt a sense of obligation to the church or its members.

Fast forward to today. The transformation of our society from an industrial age to an information/service age has created a wealth of jobs requiring a technical or bachelor's degree. After going to a college or technical school that is almost always out of our hometown, we begin searching for a job to match that education. The majority of the time the job will not be in the area where we grew up. We settle into that area and begin working on our career.

Where is the accountability now? We moved to the new location because of a job, so there are few if any close friends or relatives around us. We are more free to do as we need to insure the success of our career. Our employer has no knowledge of our "person" (character), so our value to them is based on our performance. Companies want people who get results. Individuals who can improve their bottom line, often at any cost to the well being of the employee. Risky? Of course it's risky, but the material rewards seem more important than doing what is noble. And if the employee suffers burnout or becomes ineffective because of poor character, the company can find someone else struggling to climb the ladder of success through performance.

Our focus becomes improving performance, for that is the one aspect of our life that is reinforced every day. We live in communities where a high percentage of the families are similar to us so performance becomes our source of commonality with our neighbors. "Deeper relationships can wait," we say, "I will have time to develop those later." "Virtue is its own reward," but that can be overshadowed by hearing "good job" or seeing our financial well-being increase because of our performance.

Concentrating so much on performance eventually catches up with us. Our children grow up without us being there for them. Spouses get tired of waiting on that illusive day when our focus will shift from our career to being a caring, compassionate person who sincerely desires to meet their needs instead of just pacifying them. The marriage ends in divorce or suffers harm that takes years to heal. Loved ones who were once so important in our life pass away, and we shake our heads with regret, saying, "If only I had taken more time with them." Hopefully, the void we feel in our lives will become so overwhelming that we will change our focus to "Person" before tragedy strikes.

When Lisa and I began our teaching careers, we were performance driven. We would spend 10-12 hours at our respective schools and come home exhausted. After a rushed dinner and a quick bemoaning of our days, we would begin planning for the next school day. Weekends would frequently find us at one school or the other. Even Sunday was not completely out of the picture when it came to preparing our materials and carrying out teaching-related tasks. Our spousal relationship was so intertwined with our careers it was frightening. Even time with our families was spent thinking about ways to do a better job with teaching. Our justification was that our hearts were in it for the students.

This went on for about a year and a half. We were in the process of buying a home when the deal fell through because of some unsatisfactory land use adjacent to the property. As a consolation measure to my wife, I bought her a cocker spaniel puppy. It was cute with its blonde hair and brown eyes, so precious in fact that we named her Precious. We had kept the dog about 3 days when Lisa announced that she wanted the dog housebroken. "Oh joy" I thought, "just what I need! Something else to interfere with teaching."

Housebreaking Precious required me to get up 30 minutes early each morning and walk her until she did her "business." It was November, it was cold in the morning and I hated it. After a few days, however, something strange began to happen. I actually began to enjoy walking Precious. It was not that I took great pride in seeing her perform her bodily functions; it was something else. In those few moments in the quiet of the morning, I had time to reflect on life, what I wanted to do that day, and to think about the bigger picture. Afternoons included playing with Precious and getting her to sit, stay, and fetch. I began to look forward to getting home and spending time with Lisa in the yard watching our dog. "This is what life is all about," I thought, "and I intend to experience more of the same." I am extremely thankful that it was a dog that shook me out of my performance mode instead of a newborn baby, loss of a loved one, or a failed marriage.

The ironic twist is that the development of character can make up for a lack of performance. Think about it. Think about the barber or hairdresser who may not have done a great job on your hair, but you returned to them time and time again because they were "good" persons. Or the mechanic who might occasionally miss some minute detail when repairing your car, but you would never think of going elsewhere because they are trustworthy. Then there is the insurance agent you have known for years. Even though other companies may offer better products, you would rather stay with your current policy because your agent is a "salt of the earth" kind of person.

Even in the cruel world of public speaking, character can go a long way in being accepted without a perfect performance. As a national youth officer years ago, I gave a lot of "talks" to school groups. Unfortunately, I did not always have the most eloquent or exciting things to say because I lacked training for those situations. I found, though, that if I took the time to talk with the students before or after my presentation, they responded positively to my "performance" even if it was lackluster.

One of my most troublesome presentations came in Rhode Island. At one particular high school, I was asked to visit the vocational department and share the value of vocational education. The principal escorted me to the shop and said, "Here they are." In front of me were twenty of the toughest-looking boys I think I have ever met. Many wore black leather jackets and had a look on their face that said, "Go ahead, try to make me learn. I dare you." I swallowed hard and went through the motions of my presentation, half expecting one of them to challenge me verbally. It had to be one of the worst presentations of my life. I was nervous and felt very inadequate to be talking to this group of tough guys. They were deathly silent the whole time. I asked if there were any questions, and no one raised a hand.

The shop teacher, sensing my discomfort, said, "Okay, boys, let's get to work on those engines in the shop." They immediately bolted to the shop and happily got down to business. My first instinct was to leave. They didn't care if I was there. Something told me to stay, though, so I walked into the shop and began observing the students at work. I asked them questions about their projects and inquired as to the problem with certain motors. I even took a dare from one student and attempted to pull the crank rope on an 12 horsepower motor. The force of recoil from the compression of the engine nearly broke my arm. After 15-20 minutes the principal called for me to return to the office. On my way out almost everyone of the boys thanked me for coming, and three or four even asked questions about something I had said in my presentation. Why? Because they knew *who* I was, and where I was coming from even if I could not deliver it through my words. Hence, I always try to remember the quotation, "People will never care how much you know until they know how much you care."

Rediscovering your true Character

Enough verbal slaps, huh? Me, too, my cheeks are sore. So if we have sacrificed elements of our character on the altar of performance, what is the cure? Just like Alcoholics Anonymous, the first step is to acknowledge the problem. From there you have a number of possibilities. Here are a few you might try.

1) Imagine the events that will follow your death.

This sounds morbid but can have a tremendous impact on redefining your character. Unfortunately, we will all pass from this life. Once that happens, friends and family will gather at our home and eat canned ham, fried chicken, and a hundred other things. After the initial shock has worn off and people are emotionally stable enough to talk about us, they will reminisce about who we were. It usually starts with, "Do you remember when ol' Jones..." Someone else will chime in and say, "Yeah, that's one thing about Jones. He was always..." The strange thing is that it will not be based on what we said was important in our life, but rather will be based on our actions. We will not be around to defend or clarify them, so they will stand on their own. Do you like what you hear about yourself? If not, then perhaps some changes are in order.

2) Write your character resume'
    You have just been asked to speak to a group of young people who are looking for advice on being successful. The person requesting your services asks for a resume'. It can contain no mention of your educational background, work experience, or professional achievements. The resume' can list only your character traits and examples to support your claim that the character trait did in fact reside within you.

3) Make small promises to yourself... and keep them.
    Just as "charity begins at home," so does character development. Before you radically change your life to express your true character (which leads to disappointment because it is too much at once), work on building your own trust in yourself. Make some small commitments that only you know about and work to keep them. After a few successes, it becomes easier to work on the bigger things that involve other people.
    Being a caring person has always been a character trait I have tried to carry out in my life. Four years ago when I entered public speaking full time, I got wrapped up in me, however, and let my concern for others fall by the wayside. Sadly, by the time I realized it, I had so many commitments professionally and personally that I could not immediately reverse the trend. What I did do, however, was to commit to somehow express my concern for others in the midst of my frantic world.
    The answer? I went to the local Christian bookstore and purchased a huge stack of postcards that said things like, "Thinking of you" or "Hope you feel better soon" or some similar thought. Each morning I would get up 10-15 minutes earlier than normal and quickly jot a note to 2 or 3 friends who needed encouragement. The results were astounding. I began finding myself spending 20 or 30 minutes on the task and soon found that my concern for others was again a priority

in my life instead of an afterthought. Having kept a commitment I made to myself, I now felt more comfortable making larger commitments to other people.

4) Be influenced by oranges instead of *Butterfingers*

Confused? You won't be in a minute. When my wife Lisa was pregnant, she would have chocolate cravings that could only be cured with a *Butterfinger* or similar source of chocolate. She would meander (is there a good word to describe the way an expectant mother walks) into the living room and sit down near me with her chocolate fix. Upon opening it she would say, "Jones, would you like some?" My initial response was, "No, I do not need any." Notice I said initial? After a few whiffs of that wonderful aroma, I would reply, "Uh, Lisa, I think I will have some." After one bite I would presume to be done, but the smell would come rushing back, causing me to indulge once more. Soon I had my own chocolate bar and about 400 unnecessary calories added to my waistline.

Being of sound mind, I know that an orange or some form of fruit would have been much more nutritious than a candy bar. Why don't I eat more oranges? Because no one sits in my living room eating one very often. If they did, the aroma would catch my attention when I was hungry, causing me to want one. I would then weigh several pounds less and be chock full of Vitamin C.

We cannot expect to develop good character by constantly involving ourselves with those people of poor character. Oh sure, the process is not an immediate one but rather a gradual one. It may start with a fellow employee telling you how they embellish their expense voucher. You would never do such a thing, right? Continue to hang around that person and their influence, and you may soon say, "Well, maybe just this once." After the first time it becomes easier because the influence that helped you deviate the first time is still there, prodding you again. You take a second helping and soon find yourself doing something you never dreamed possible a short time earlier.

A few years ago my wife and I helped start a new United Methodist Church. It has been one of the most humbling experiences of our life because of the impact the church has had on so many people. Early in our church history, however, a couple entered our church and began causing problems. They wanted to verbally rip apart much of the minister's actions and questioned the sincerity of some people within the church. My wife and I had refused to be a part of other churches with many people like that, and we stayed out of their line of fire.

Because of an accident, I became homebound for a couple weeks. During that time the couple brought a meal and stayed for what seemed like hours. As I listened to them talk, my view toward them softened, and I actually began to feel sorry for them. Maybe what they were saying did make sense. After a couple of phone conversations, I became convinced that their perceptions had some validity. I approached our pastor and confronted him with the same charges that a few weeks before I had said were ridiculous. His first comment was, "Have you been talking with _____?" At that point I shook with the realization that I had been worn down over time. I apologized for being shallow and made sure I stayed clear of those individuals. They soon left the church, and we were all better for it.

The flip side of this is that we can improve our character by associating ourselves with those who are "orange-like" in their character. We simply have to seek them out and make a commitment (that word seems to be popping up often) to learn from their example.

A Parting Word
"Make your life visual, not verbal." Character is rarely verbal unless someone is describing yours. The ultimate expression of our character resides in our day-to-day actions.

D

Decisions

In the book *Alice in Wonderland*, Alice comes to a fork in the road. She asks the Cheshire Cat which way she should go. The cat responds, "Where do you wish to go?" Alice responds, "Oh! It really doesn't matter." The cat replies, "Then it really doesn't make any difference which way you go!" To me that sums up most people's decision-making process. Failure to consider where one wants a decision to take them creates a crisis because there are no scales on which to weigh the merits of one choice over another. Complicating the process even more is the perception given by society that it is your business and you should look only at the effect it will have on your happiness for the moment. Look at TV shows. No matter what choices are made by the participants in the situation comedy or drama, most of the time everything falls into place by the time the credits roll. We like movies that have deep conflict and suspense AS LONG AS all problems are solved by the time we exit the theatre. I remember feeling torn at the end of *Platoon*, a movie about the Vietnam War. Most war movies end with a hero or group of heroes who preserve our belief that war is a clear battle between good and evil. Vietnam, however, was a different war, and the movie was (by critics' reviews) a fairly accurate portrayal. Too many decisions were not clear, and the outcomes not always honorable, which rubbed against my "happily ever after" mentality.

Here are some other reasons people make "bonehead" (translated "poor") decisions:

1) They want to make sure they have all the information. Making decisions includes using your common sense based on pertinent information, and visualizing your desired outcome. Waiting for just the right information to hit you like a Mac truck and jolt you into a decision rarely happens.

2) Indecision is a decision. Failure to choose one course of direction or another constitutes a decision. It's like sitting at an intersection looking at a roadmap, trying to determine your best route to a specific location. The longer you sit idle, the more fuel you burn and time you waste. If you sit long enough, you may not have time to reach your destination or you may lack the energy (fuel) necessary to get there.

3) The decision must please everyone. Seesaw personalities (see personality chapter) drive me crazy with this one. An acceptable decision to them is one in which all parties involved are in total agreement. Unless we are all dying of thirst and the watering hole is right in front of us, don't expect total agreement on anything. Besides, who gets to drink first?

4) Emotions are powerful. Commercials appeal to every sense of emotion in our beings to get us to buy their product. This soft drink will make you feel like skydiving, that car will make all your worries go away (except for the car payment), or this cake can be eaten with no concern about calories (they fail to mention that it tastes like cardboard). People manipulate others with emotional pleas. The guy should have sexual relations with the girl because she loves him. You should feel a certain way toward that person because you are my friend.

Framework for Making Decisions

"Okay, Mr. Wise Guy," you are saying, "if you're so doggoned smart, tell me a way to make decisions more effectively." It would be my honor. Just remember one thing: These are merely thoughts based on my own good and one or two bad decisions. You have to choose the process that works best for you.

1) Start with your values. We have devoted a whole chapter to a discussion of values, so I will not go into detail here other than to say this is an area overlooked by many people. Our values, if genuine, offer a multitude of information that can serve as a reference point in making decisions.

Lisa and I had two very different first teaching experiences. Mine was fantastic while hers was a constant battle. Never before have I felt so helpless in my life. I would get out of bed anticipating a great day with my students while Lisa could only look forward to the day being over. After two years, Lisa had had all she could take. The problem was, what could we do? Finding two school systems in close proximity to each other that needed agricultural teachers would be next to impossible. Besides, *I* was happy. Maybe she could find something else in the area, and I could continue to enjoy my teaching situation. What it came down to for me, however, was my values. One of my values is to have a successful marriage. Part of that value includes the phrase, "I work constantly for the good of 'us' and am not afraid to sacrifice my needs for our needs." Getting Lisa into a better teaching situation would definitely improve our marriage because Lisa could again be the self-confident, caring person I knew she wanted to be, but was not so worn down by her current situation. We found Lisa a better place, and she went on to five outstanding years in education, making an impact on many students, teachers and community members. You might wonder what to do if a decision impacts more than one of your values. We will talk about ranking your values in order of importance later.

2) Compare your decision to a financial investment. When investing money, you want to invest it where you will get the greatest return. Does one decision offer a greater return on your investment (improved relations with others, personal well being, career advancement) than another? Remember, if your chosen area of investment (decision) actually costs you something (quality of relationship, personal harm, career jeopardy), you will have to make several good decisions (investments) to recoup the losses from the one bad one.

3) What impact will your decision have on:

Your health	*Your family*	*Your friends*
Your career	*Your financial security*	*Your reputation*

Thus far in my young life I have made four life changing decisions:

- To accept Christ
- To marry Lisa
- To have a child (made in cooperation with Lisa)
- To become a professional speaker

This is not to say there were not some other extremely important ones, but these have forever altered the course of my life. To prevent a pool of tears from showering my keyboard, I will refrain from discussing the first three. The fourth one stirs great emotion but of a kind that I can type about without breaking out the tissue box. (I cry at mushy TV commercials.)

The decision to enter public speaking full time was one that I wrestled with for a long time. Going from being a secure public school teacher to a job that offered only the security of knowing that everything depended on me scared me to death. I wanted to pursue it, but the uncertainty was something I could live without. It was once again my wife who helped me look at the big picture. She said, "Let's look at the effect your decision will have on our life."

My health. The impact on my physical health would be minimal, but what about my mental health. I had been greatly frustrated with teaching, not because of the students, but rather by the fact that I spent so little time working with students and so much time with paper work and other non-instructional duties. Going into business for myself would alleviate many of those frustrations because now the harder I worked on being successful in the business, the more time I would be given to work with students and adults in keynotes and workshops.

My family. My immediate family (Lisa) would be negatively affected because she would become the major breadwinner for two years (the time needed for most businesses to begin turning a profit). However, she would be helped in the sense that she could now devote more attention to her preparations for school because I would be working out of the home and could keep the clothes washed, meals cooked, and errands completed. That would also allow her to rest more when at home, which, unknown at the time, would become extremely important with her future pregnancy.

My friends. I saw no immediate impact on my relationship to my friends, so this did not play into my decision.

My career. A little more soul searching had to take place here. What if the business failed? Could I return to teaching? The answer seemed to be yes because over the past three years there had been at least one agriculture teaching vacancy in a 25-mile radius. My teaching certification was current through 1999, so I was covered in this area.

My (Our) financial well being. A long time ago we had been given sound advice on money management (see chapter by the same name) and were basically living off one income while saving the rest. Even though our public speaking business could not support us now, I could (and did) substitute when I was available as well as take other odd jobs to keep a cushion in our income.

My reputation. Originally, this one area bugged me more than anything. How could I face other people if my new venture failed? What would they say about me? Once again, my wife was the voice of reason as she said, "What can they say? At least you were out there trying to reach your dreams. What about all the people who never try?"

Armed with all these answers, the decision became clear. Clear, but not easy. Remember, though, nothing ventured, nothing gained.

4) Do you have the support systems in place to help you honor your decision?

If walking a financial tightrope will be required, do you have a family or bank net in place to catch you? If you will need extra child care, can you rely on your friends? What if you need an inexpensive source of labor to do anything from run errands to answer a phone to mow your lawn? When you get frustrated or lose your way, will there be individuals you can rely on who will get you back on track without saying, "I told you so?" Lastly, if there will come a definite time to acknowledge your decision was a bad one, are there people in your life you trust and respect enough to allow them to be a type of conscientious observer?

After the decision has been made, expect buyer's remorse to play a factor in your thoughts. Studies have indicated that after purchasing any item of significance (for some it might be a watch, for others, a car or 100 acres of land), we all experience a period of buyer's remorse. During this time we intensely question the validity of our decision, and any negative repercussions or incidents (car does not perform as planned, land is found to have a problem with pine beetles) cause us to scream, "I have messed up big time."

In my opinion there are two ways to minimize buyer's remorse. The first is to make the decision and then make it right. We return to our opening statement once again. Once a decision is made, you have to work to optimize the benefits of the decision and minimize the negative implications of it. Remember, Will Rogers said, "Even if you are on the right track you will get run over if you do not move." A seemingly obvious right decision can become a wrong one if we do not put effort into supporting it. What happens if you take a new job? Do you say, "Okay, I made the right decision. Now I can rest." No! You work harder than ever to insure that the job will work out.

A perfect example of making a decision and making it right is deciding to get married. Couples walk into life with a gleam in their eyes and bird seed in their hair. Bliss is bountiful, and husband and wife settle in for a wonderful experience. They work on their careers, their friendships, and even their home. They fail, however, to spend time working on their marriage. Spending quality time together and meeting each other's needs come in a distant second or third to other things ("I will get to it later"). Children come into the picture, and the already-strained marriage sinks even deeper into frustration. "Where is that tremendous bond we felt so long ago?" they ask. The answer? Even the strongest bonds can be destroyed if not constantly checked and repaired after the storms of career pressures, children and feelings of isolation.

While I was growing up, there was one couple whom I loved to watch. Sue and Chester Parker were permanent honeymooners. You never talked to one or the other very long without hearing them sing the praises of their spouse. When they were together, you could tell they *were* together. They would hold hands and have that special grin on their face that said, "I'm in love." My mother talked to Ms. Parker one day and asked about their lasting marriage. "Well, I'll just tell you. Chester and I have always worked on our marriage. Sometimes it was tempting to let our children come between us, but we knew that if we were going to make it, we had to keep our marriage as one of the cornerstones of our life. We love our children, grandchildren, and great grandchildren dearly, but Chester comes first, and I know he feels the same way about me." In life, when you make a decision, you must *make* it right.

You can make the choice to go to college and feel great about your decision. If, however, you let your grades slip in high school or fail to apply yourself once enrolled in college, that right decision does not seem so right anymore. I have made the decision to lose weight countless times but gulping down a bowl of fudge ripple ice cream before bed does not honor that decision.

The second way to minimize buyer's remorse is to answer this question: "At what point will I know if this decision was a good or bad one?" Establishing your answer to this question now before the emotional influences seep into the situation will assist in giving you some "stick-to-itiveness." It reminds me of my mother-in-law's attitude toward recreational gambling. When she and my father-in-law go on a cruise they have a set amount they will sacrifice to the one arm bandits. If they make money, great. If they lose it all, they will spend no more. Setting boundaries like that helps them reap the benefits of their decision (enjoyment from playing the slot machines) while establishing a logical point to walk away. Many Las Vegas gamblers have been wiped out because they made the decision to "try their luck" but depended only on their emotions to serve as a guide.

If your decision is to get a college education, the answer may come when you secure (or can not secure) a job related to your major. Perhaps you choose to invest in the stock market. Your point of revelation comes when your investment has grown 10% or when you have lost all your money. A new job? You may choose to deem it a good or bad decision after giving it six months or when your blood pressure reaches panic levels. Choosing to buy or lease a new automobile may be in your future plans. At what point will you be able to evaluate whether the decision was a good one? Will it be when you have to stop buying food for your family? Maybe it will come when you no longer have to go to the chiropractor after taking a long road trip with your family. Establishing your boundaries early may serve to smooth out the speed bumps brought on by buyer's remorse.

Now go make some decisions...and make them right.

Even after all this stuff, your tendency may still be to allow indecision to be your decision. To me a bad decision is better than no decision. Relatively few decisions in our lives are actually life-threatening or totally irreversible. Those types of decisions often have to be made because of a poor decision or series of decisions made earlier in life.

How about a lesson from nature? Locate a river in your area and follow it upstream toward its source. (If you live near the Mississippi River, and plan to follow it to its source, take this book with you...along with a whole lot of supplies.... you are going to be gone for a while.) What do you notice about the width of the river in relation to the source? Obviously, the river will be narrower closer to its origin. For our teachable moment today class, tell me: Where will it be easier to cross the river, upstream or downstream?

Imagine that the river is time and the riverbank on the other side represents a decision to be made. Since you can not go back in time (move upstream), you can either cross where you are or continue walking down river hoping for a few rocks, fallen trees, or a shallow section to make it easier for you to cross. Will they be there? Who knows? What if you're stranded on this side because of your age or circumstances?

Go on, soak your shoes, splash on across the river. The journey is not going to get any easier.

E

Educating with Excellence

Yes, this chapter is on public speaking. However, our primary focus will not be on the development of "killer" (a youth term used in place of "outstanding") speeches or simply creating seminars or workshops with magnificent content and immortal impact. As soon as I figure out how to do that every time I speak, I will write another book, and you can buy it. Instead, this chapter looks at inputs over which you have a great deal of control regardless of your oral presentation skills. I think the proper term is the mechanics of the presentation.

Why this direction? As I travel, people always want pointers or tips about being a more effective presenter. In my opinion, the only way to improve your actual presentation skills is to practice. In her book *Speak and Grow Rich*, Dottie Walters coined the phrase, "Go from free to shining fee." What she meant was that the primary way to become a successful speaker (in terms of money) is to take every opportunity to speak, which often means speaking for free. As your skills improve, your fee can increase as well. Practicing in front of a mirror may help with hand gestures or content familiarity, but it can not duplicate the actual speaking environment.

What *can* be learned, however, without a great deal of practice, is how to set up a meeting room for maximum effect with your audience, what to do if the group is unresponsive, and other similar items. Frequently, just altering the temperature in the room can have a dramatic impact on the attitude of the audience. When I conduct workshops or seminars with young people or adults, the first thing I do when I walk into my meeting room is to find the thermostat. If it is at all warm, I do all I can to get it cool in the room. Why? Because we are all so busy these days that when we sit down for a few minutes, our bodies yearn for sleep. Participants at professional development conferences stay up late socializing (and a host of other things) and arrive at the seminar already drowsy. Getting the room cool, along with a number of other things which will be discussed later, can make or break the quality of your presentation, regardless of your content.

Granted, you may not always be able to make the necessary mechanical changes to improve your setting, or it may be better to leave things well enough alone. Once, while trying to improve the lighting in a ballroom where 1000 conventioneers were preparing to listen to my keynote, I accidentally blew the fuse on one entire side of the conference center. They really do need to put better labels on those switches in the "Employees Only" room. If, however, you have an abundance of strategies to use to enhance audience effect, you can usually implement at least one or two.

Room Set Up for Maximum Effect

Different meetings and activities call for varying room set ups. The following are some basic room arrangements, with their strengths or weaknesses.

Theater: Chairs are in strict rows from left to right and front to back. With the exception of putting the participants on the floor, this setup gets the maximum number of people into a room. It is most commonly used for convention sessions where all of the activity will be in front of the group in a specific area.

Classroom: Desks or tables are arranged in straight rows. This style works okay if no other arrangement can be made. It creates a rigid structure allowing for minimal interaction among participants.

"V" Classroom: Tables are arranged in an open "V" formation in one or more rows. This style works well when a focal point is necessary (i.e. overhead, TV/VCR, LCD projector) and information needs to be written down. It also allows for more interaction among participants because they can see each other more easily.

Conference: Chairs arranged around a table or some similar fashion where participants are facing each other. Group interaction is encouraged, but numbers should remain around 15 or less. Higher numbers will prevent participants from adequately hearing or seeing each other. This style is most appropriate when participants are working on a group project.

Curved Theater: Chairs are arranged in curved rows similar to a crescent moon. It is a great alternative to the standard theater set up. Interaction is encouraged by the curved shape. The presenter can also remain closer to more members of the group than in a conventional theatre setup.

Campfire: No chairs are used. Participants sit on the floor in a half moon shape or circle. The informalness of this style encourages conversation among participants and removes some formality barriers created by other styles. If groups get too large (25 or more), the intimacy of the setting can be lost because of the difficulty in hearing.

Other Items to Consider
- Have handouts at each station or seat before the meeting unless they need to be given out at an appropriate time.
- Remove as many distractions as possible in the room. Doors that show people passing by or allow noises to filter into the room are common sources of annoyance. Windows showing a beautiful day or other activities outside can distract the focus of even the most ardent seminar participant.
- If a noisy group is anticipated, increase the distance between chairs adjacent to each other. It makes it more difficult to carry on a conversation with someone nearby.

- If you are in a room that is larger than you need, remove extra chairs or place them away from your area. People will fill the space allotted to them.
- If you are in an auditorium that is larger than you need, place a strip of masking tape along the entrance to rows you will not need.
- If the temperature of the room can be adjusted, make the room slightly cool to keep the presenter (you) and the participants alert.
- If available, use a microphone unless it reduces the quality of your presentation. I wish I had a dime for every instance when a presenter said, "I don't need that microphone... I have a big mouth." In the ensuing presentation, though, the level of their voice would decrease so much that the first one or two rows were the only ones graced by their powerful words. It is just not natural for most people (except coaches and parents) to talk at a high volume for a long period of time. Use the microphone.

Are They Climbing the Walls or Cowering in the Corners?

Just before beginning your presentation, you sense that your group is a little quiet and reserved. Oh well, those 15 opening questions you were going to wow them with can be tossed out the window. What will you do now? Then there's the group of 50 that sounds like 500. Just getting them to sit down will be a miracle. Do you really want to open your presentation with a 15-minute monologue? You would be better off sharing your words of wisdom with a group of 3-year-olds after their afternoon nap and 3 chocolate bars. They would be much more receptive.

One of my proudest moments thus far in public speaking came at a middle school in South Carolina. I was asked to be there as a part of Drug Education Week. I arrived around 12:30 PM and was escorted to the gymnasium. Walking in the doors, you could feel the energy. Wall to wall students ranging in age from 10 to 13. The students had just finished lunch and were pumped full of sugar and caffeine. It was a rainy day, which seems to make all students a little more active. Topping it all off was the fact that my presence had interrupted their schedule, which is like adding fuel to a fire. One of the teachers came over and said, "Sir, I pity you." Perplexed, I said, "Excuse me?" She said, "I pity you." "Why?" I asked. She replied, "Forty-five minutes with this crowd? You are in trouble." I merely grinned and began my presentation. What followed was one of my best programs to a school group. Why? Through the years I had learned several ways to bring an audience "down" and to channel their energy into my presentation instead of trying to avoid it. We finished the program on a high note, and the students left the gymnasium as energetic as when they had arrived. I approached the teacher who had shared her comments with me and said, "Ma'am, I pity you." Confused, she said, "What do you mean?" I replied, "Just what I said. I pity you because I may have had them for 45 minutes, but you've got them the rest of the afternoon. Have a great day." One of these days my smart alec wit is going to get me into real trouble.

If your group looks to be active (i.e. noisy and/or energetic):
Before your presentation begins:
- Adjust the seating (see Room Set Up)
- Stand at the door and make eye contact
- Talk with many as possible about their interests and activities. When you ask them to settle down later, they will have a greater respect for you since you took the time to listen to them.

During the Presentation:
- Start the session on time. Doing this lets people know you obviously have important stuff to do. Also, people have become accustomed to starting meetings late, and several people may not even be in the room yet. Working with the ones who are in the room will help set the tone for the ones who will enter the room later. You do not actually have to start imparting information. You can tell a joke, give background information about yourself, or point out the location of the nearest rest rooms.

- Begin with a total group activity. You can expend a large amount of their energy just by getting them up and moving around. When working with adults, my favorite activity is "If You." It works like this. Ask a general question like, "If your favorite food is steak, move to this part of the room." Ask about other foods and have them move to corresponding parts of the room. You can use sports teams, hobbies, or any common areas of interest. Now that you have them in small groups, give them a question to answer within that group. If your topic is Public Speaking, ask each of them to respond to the statement, "My greatest fear in public speaking is..." You get several benefits from this activity: 1) The participants discover commonalties among their group, 2) They expend some of their energy by laughing and standing up for a few minutes, and 3) You get the chance to adjust your presentation if necessary. When all groups are finished, allow them to return to their seats.

- Ask general open-ended questions and get individual responses. Doing so encourages the group to be respective of other members and listen to their responses.

- Change direction and type of activities often. For adults, the average attention span is about 7-10 minutes. Why? Guess how long it is between commercials on TV? Yep, 7-10 minutes. This does not mean you have to actually get them out of their seats each time (don't wear them out), you just need to interject a new idea, change from the overhead to a dry erase board, ask a question, tell a joke, or do something to keep them alert.

- Keep a fast pace throughout the program. Active groups typically can be kept in check by moving at such a pace that they have to pay attention. Notice that I did not say you need to talk fast. It is the information and activities that you want to push along at a fast pace.

- Move to the noisy area while speaking. This tends to be more effective with youth, but just walking by a group of noisy adults will sometimes give a subtle hint.

- Talk professionally and/or use humor with the people causing the problem by saying:
"I'm sorry, did you want to add something?"
"You sure are an energetic individual. What did you have for lunch? (breakfast, snack, etc.)"

If your group tends to be quiet (reluctant to talk or participate):
Before the presentation begins:
• Adjust seating to encourage audience interaction (see Room Setup)

• Get to know one or two people who arrive early. Doing so will give you a couple of strong allies once your program has begun. After the others see the ease with which you talk to your early participants, they will warm up much more quickly.

• Talk with as many participants as possible to break the ice.

During the presentation:
• Have participants introduce themselves to one other person near them. If possible, don't even have them to get up. Remember, warm them up gradually.

• Have a humorous activity early involving 1 or 2 volunteers (or your allies from earlier). Getting a good laugh from the entire audience can jumpstart even the most reserved group.

• Use a total group activity later in the program. Using one early may make the participants feel uncomfortable.

• Ask fill-in-the-blank group questions at first and move gradually to open-ended ones. For example, if your topic is Time Management, you might say, "One phrase we all use is that we will have time for that _____." Getting them in the habit of talking will help later as you break out in smaller groups or ask open-ended questions.

• Relax your manner of presentation. Sit on the edge of a table or desk. Soften your voice from time to time.

Finishing up

Following all these steps may not make you an overnight success but can assist you in creating presentations that maintain people's interest and allow you to maintain a level of sanity before and during the program. Who knows? You can probably even give me some pointers.

Focus

Busy? Okay, dumb question. Feeling stressed out because you can't seem to get it all done? Our parents did. Our grandparents did, too. Somehow, though, we have succeeded in having more stuff to do than ever before. Time management (discussed briefly in another chapter) systems or "planners," as they are called, are hotter than ever. Magazines at the grocery store check-out line scream for us to buy them because they offer ways to help us get more done in less time. Bookstores are filled with self-help materials that tell us how to keep our lives between the guard rails and get to that all-elusive destination of contentment. Schools struggle to hold the attention of students. More young people than ever are diagnosed with Attention Deficit Disorder, and teachers are constantly being bombarded with ways to be more diverse in their teaching methods. Where have we missed the boat? Why do we have such a difficult time focusing on the important issues in our life? Here are some possible reasons:

Technology is a blessing *and* a curse.

Telephones/beepers/pagers/e Mail: Ten years ago, our primary means of communication was still a telephone attached to a wall jack. If you were away from the phone, someone would just have to wait until you were close enough to the phone to hear it ring to get in touch with you. Mail was of the "snail" kind, and you could figure a period of 3-5 days for information to reach the other party. Time driving in cars and waiting in doctor's offices or grocery lines were moments to reflect on events of the day or to plan for your next assignment or errand because no one could get to you to interrupt your train of thought.

What about today? If properly equipped with a beeper, you can be reached anywhere...and I do mean anywhere. On a flight recently, I laughed as one sleeping passenger was rudely awakened by an annoyed person in the seat next to him who informed him that his pager had been beeping for the last 5 minutes. Have a cell phone with you, and you can not only be interrupted but can call and interrupt other people. By the looks of all the phones growing out of people's ears while driving, we take full advantage of our chance to bother someone else.

Don't get me wrong. Communications technology has its place, but all these audible (or vibrating) interruptions are destroying our ability to focus. Think about it. You are in deep thought about an important project or in a critical conversation with an employee or family member. Your beeper goes off. Even if it simply vibrates, your attention is drawn to that interruption. "Who is it?" you wonder. Oops, what did the other person just say? If you look to see the number of the person calling, your mind drifts even further away because you ponder what they are calling about. "Oops, did they just tell me to do something?"

Procrastinators have greatly benefited from all these gadgets. Before, if they had a problem or project that needed some focused thought, travel or wait time forced them to begin the process. Now, they can politely avoid it by using their cell phone and getting their mind on something of less importance but greater satisfaction.

Fax/e-mail: If the problem was not bad enough, these two wonderful devices offer more opportunities to minimize focus time. Need information? We can fax it to you immediately. Then I will call you (and leave a message on your voice mail) and we can discuss it.

Then there's e-mail. Once again our procrastinators revel in this device because they can avoid an unpleasant project by checking their e-mail. "There might be something important," they reason. Right. Someone lost an earring and wants to know if anyone on the fifth floor has found it. Or here's the latest joke. Remember, if it were *that* important, they would have called you or dialed your beeper.

Television/VCR: Once upon a time televisions had these little knobs you turned to get a different station. I actually stayed in a hotel recently that had TVs with them, which tells you about the budget of some of my groups. If you did not like what was on, you would put up with it until you got the energy to go turn the knob, or someone walked through the room and you manipulated them into doing it for you. Today, you can change channels at a moment's notice as often as you like. Add to that cable, direct TV, or the like, and you have unlimited opportunities to change your mind about what to watch. If you are still not satisfied, pop a tape into the VCR.

Some of you are worried about me. "He sounds like the 'unabomber's manuscript' with all this anti-technology ranting and raving," you say. No, I enjoy the convenience of many of these items but fear that they have eliminated most opportunities for quality, private thinking, especially if we are not intentional about finding time for it. Retreats for everyone from church officers to county commissioners to corporate executives are seen as a way to "get away from it all" and focus on the challenges facing the organization or institution.

2) We may be suffering from information overload.

Following an isolated food poisoning scare in the Western part of the United States, a weekend news magazine published a list of the fears of Americans. While only a small percentage of people actually get poisoned from eating poorly prepared foods, the percentage of Americans concerned about food poisoning was over thirty percent. Why? Because it had been paraded in front of our eyes so much in the past few weeks. Six months from now it will have faded dramatically unless another similar situation occurs again. But wait, shouldn't our concern be the same all the time? Well, of course, you say. Why isn't it? We can only handle a limited number of crises at one time. I'll put food poisoning back on my crisis list next week. Right now, there is a hole in the ozone problem that I need to fret over.

3) We train ourselves to believe "we can do it all."

Take a moment and list all the roles you fulfill in your life. Yes, really take a moment and at least mentally complete the activity. If you need a second sheet of paper, just rip out one of the blank ones at the end of this book. My partial list looks like this:

Husband	*Father*	*Son*
Breadwinner	*Speaker*	*Neighbor*
Playmate for daughter	*Friend*	*Church Member*
Son in Law	*Sunday School Teacher*	

Now for each role list some of your responsibilities. Your head is swelling as you realize just how many responsibilities you juggle and still remain sane (at least part of the time).

One of my seminars is entitled *Time Management and You.* In that seminar individuals begin with a look at their roles and attempt to define them more clearly. At the first break, a few rather agitated individuals will approach me and say, "This all sounds good, but I have so many people counting on me. I just do not see how I can meet all my obligations." My answer, "You can't!" That was not the answer they were looking for. They wanted some magical way to squeeze more time out of their day (like getting a baby doll away from my daughter). As a society we have attempted to schedule, scan, plan and ponder every possible way to fill every moment in our day, and if we don't we feel guilty about it.

"Conveniences were supposed to solve this problem," you say. From food preparation to communications to the increased speed limit, every facet of our world is loaded with things to make our lives simpler and more manageable. Instead we have chosen to manage more stuff and found ourselves right back at ground zero. Instead of "Work smarter, not harder" we have chosen to "Work smarter and then work some more with that extra time."

Lisa and I struggle to find friends our age (late 20's to mid 30's) who are not spread thin in their lives. If we do manage to have a meal or a little social time with them, we hear of all the things they have got to get done later, the next day, or in the near future. It can almost be depressing because you sense that they would like to stop the madness but just do not know where to begin. They remind me of someone plugging holes in a barrel filled with water. One hole emerges, and they use their index finger. Another hole is plugged with the other index finger. Next, a hole develops on the other side. They stretch as much as possible and finally manage to reach it with their big toe. This continues until they have nothing left to plug a hole with and can do no better than to just try and slow the rate of water leaving the barrel.

Focusing your mind

Turn off the TV, radio, and/or computer. Silence. Say the word again...silence. Why don't we search for silence more often? In my opinion silence scares us. In those quiet moments our minds relentlessly search for something to be distracted by in order to avoid focusing on major issues in our life. Music is a source of relaxation for people, and works wonderfully. But even music can frequently divert our focus from matters at hand that need serious attention.

When you get into your car, turn the radio off. There's some time to focus your mind on what needs to be done. Take out the TV guide once a week and plan your viewing schedule. Leaving the TV off when you are not actively watching it will encourage your mind to focus.

Much of my time travelling requires hotel stays. Upon entering the room I normally turn the TV on and search for my favorite station, *CMT* (Country Music Television). We don't have cable at our house (see chapter on money management), and the only time I get to watch *CMT* Videos is when I travel. Normally, I will spend part of the evening reviewing my program for the next day, looking for ways to tweak or adjust it for maximum effect. I leave the TV on, reassuring myself that, "I'll just leave it on for the noise." Soon my attention is skewed, and I find nothing to change about my program. If I turn off the TV, however, and just focus on the program, I find my brain developing all types of new ideas and thoughts. Why didn't they leap out before? They were almost there, but were beaten back by the desire to see the last few clips of a Reba McEntire video.

Even with Alex (2.5 years old), I have been introduced to the power of TV. Alex is a wonderful child who will eat almost anything (a chip off the ol' block). If she decides that a new food is not delectable, we have devised a way to get her to eat it. Place her on the couch and turn on a children's video. Slowly spoon the recently rejected food into her mouth, and she will normally eat it. What's the difference? When she was sitting at the table, she was concentrating on what she was eating. Distract her, however, and almost anything can be passed across her lips. Perhaps children's videos would not work with an adult, but there are other programs that draw our attention away from matters at hand, and cause us to waste valuable time. Time that we *say* is valuable, but do not show it with our actions. (Review character chapter)

Focusing your life

Rip your life into little pieces. "It's already there," you sneer. Good, you are one step ahead of the rest of us. No, seriously, get some small sheets of paper and a pen. On each sheet of paper write one of the roles you have in your life. Having done that, find a place where you can be reflective with your thoughts. Go out to your car after everyone has gone to bed. Find a room in your house where you can be alone (yes, even the bathroom will work). Ask yourself this question: "If I had to drop one of these roles in my life, I would take away..." Take that role and place it in a pile by itself. Ask yourself the question again and choose another role to take away. Yes, you know where this is going, but keep it up until all the roles are in a stack.

You now have your roles in order of importance for the moment. Notice I added "for the moment." Our roles are dynamic, and therefore we have to be in a constant state of evaluation about which role is most important for us to fulfill today, this week, or even next month. When I return home from a road trip, my role as a spouse and father take center stage. If it does not, you know what happens. If it's Saturday evening and I have not completed my preparation for Sunday School class, the role of teacher takes precedence. Perhaps you are not so involved as to actually sit down with your list of roles and repeat this exercise (although it might be a good idea). Completing it mentally, however, may go a long way toward restoring some order to your life when things go haywire.

Summation

Ever heard of Vaudeville? In the first half of this century one popular form of entertainment included individual or groups of men who would come on stage, tell jokes, sing, dance, or do any number of other things to entertain an audience. One of my favorite acts was the plate spinner. He would line up several sticks or small poles and then, one by one, place plates on them and start them spinning. After adding about 3 or 4 he would have to return to the first ones and spin them more to keep them from falling. I was amazed to see him sometimes get up to 15 or 20 plates spinning at one time without falling. He had not a moment's rest, however, because he had to constantly spin this one a little, then over here a moment, and then to another one.

Ever feel like that? Does it seem like your life is one continuous struggle to keep things spinning? Jumping from one role in your life to another, giving it just enough of your time and energy to keep it propped up for a few moments while you rush to another one? Maybe it's time to look seriously at how many plates (roles) you have spinning and think about taking a few down so you can concentrate on the ones that are most important to you.

"But so many people are counting on me," you reply. Okay, maybe they are. If that's the case, then perhaps a look at air travel will help bring the issue into...yes, focus. When travelling by air (plane, that is), one is told that in an emergency, oxygen masks will fall from the ceiling. You are to place the mask on your face and breath normally (yeah, right). If you are travelling with a small child, however, you should put the mask over your face first and then over the face of the child. Get the picture? If we are to put ourselves in a position to help others or be effective in our relationships with them, we must first focus on getting our own lives in order.

G

Goals

Probably the most over-used expression in professional and personal development presentations is "setting goals." "Set your goals high," they say, and you can accomplish anything. True, goals are the backbone of personal or professional growth because they force us to do better than before. After telling others to set goals, the typical next step is to highlight individuals who have overcome great obstacles to reach their goals. Lastly, we encourage others to decide what they want in life and set goals related to those ambitions. The process sounds valid, but a few potholes in the road to success seem to emerge.

First, goals are so often geared toward "getting" we forget about "being." With young people, a common goal is to get married to a wonderful individual or to get a good-paying job. These are seemingly solid directions to take with one's life, but if the focus is on getting, then the results can be less than satisfying. Men, perhaps your goal is to get married to a rich, beautiful woman whose father will pay for your every need. The end result seems perfect. I use the word "seems", however, because what happens if the money runs out or you and your spouse have trouble communicating and getting along? Right, find another rich woman. Then you can join the countless ranks of other adults who have made the same mistake. Why? Because the goal to "be a good spouse" probably never materialized in their minds until they did irreparable damage to the relationship.

When the focus is on getting, the keys to the goal seem to focus on events and circumstances that are often outside of our complete control. If, however, the focus is on *being* something, the responsibility falls squarely back onto our shoulders. During my first year of teaching I had in my class a student who wanted to go to NC State University (be still my beating heart) to get a degree in Veterinary Medicine. I loved to hear Jim share his knowledge of animal science with others and just knew he would be a successful veterinarian one day. Unfortunately, Jim never made it to NC State in the Veterinary Medicine program. His grades fell during his first two years of high school, and by the time he was a junior he was struggling simply to pass some of his classes. He had the intelligence, social skills, and even the financial support (a big plus in today's college costs) to make it. He failed because he chose not to focus on being a good student. At last report, he was wandering from job to job, failing to settle on a single direction.

Secondly, each day is a step in getting closer or further away from your goal. When you got up this morning, did you think about your goals in life? Ha! you say. Just getting to work on time was a major achievement for me. Gee, you sound like me some time ago. I have always been the type of person who liked to get up early and get things done in the morning (Lisa is not, and that has been the source of many interesting discussions). When teaching, I would always be at work by 7:00 AM. During my last year of teaching, however, my routine changed because my goals in life were changing. Wanting to go into business for myself, I found that my motivation to get to school early was gone. Even though I still wanted to be a good teacher in those remaining months, I just did not have the extra "Oomph" needed to arrive at school early. Lisa, although worried about me, enjoyed the few extra minutes of sleep as now my plan became, "How late can I leave for school and still be ready for class?" A paradox had formed because what I was working for was not one of my main goals in life, and working as a teacher was pushing me further away from my goal because it was time that could be spent developing our business. Lisa and I had begun to talk about having children, and I knew that once they (we only have one; the jury is still out on a second one) were on the scene, venturing into such an unsure world as self-employment would be almost out of the question.

Surprisingly enough, upon leaving teaching, the desire to arise early and get the worm (what an incentive) returned. Part of that, you say, is a result of the fact that you must make ends meet. Yes, that would be a major incentive since one of my values is to be financially successful. But on a deeper level, I am actively engaged in a profession in which I want to *succeed.* Every day becomes a new opportunity to learn about my profession and hone my skills, and if I want to succeed, I must take what each day brings to become a more effective speaker.

The failure of people to realize the need to actively engage in thinking about their goals is most recognizable in matters of money management. We all know people who are constantly joking (they are really serious, though) about a lack of money in their life. "I need a job that makes more money" or "If we didn't have so many bills we could make ends meet." There *are* many instances when the amount of money flowing into the family coffers are insufficient, but sometimes it may be the excessive amount that flows out over a year in very small increments. One culprit is the infamous plastic bottle of soft drink (soda, pop, drink or whatever your culture calls it). Confused? Read on.

In the chapter on money management we will discuss the frivolous areas of spending that can make or break us, so we will limit our discussion to the plastic bottle at this point. As one comedian said, "When did America become so thirsty?" Everywhere you look people are carrying around those 16 ounce, 20 ounce, or even 1 liter bottles of soft drink or bottled water. It has become a common practice to grab one when visiting a convenience store while going on a trip of more than 5 minutes. They are popular in schools where they can be carried in a back pack and partaken of at will. To my dismay, one human resources director, talking to a group of high school students, even told them not to bring those bottles into an interview. Excuse me? Inquiring later, I found that several individuals actually did lug the bottles of soda nectar into their interview. Perhaps it was to show their choice of a quality soft drink (which would work well if they were interviewing for a job at a soda bottling plant). Yes, it could be those bottles of natural spring water or some form of H_2O that has been flavored for one of a hundred different tastes.

Getting down from my soap box now, I must return to the point at hand. These bottles of soda are expensive when purchased individually. Let's do the math. If they cost 75 cents each, and you purchase one 4 days a week (got up too late one morning to stop), that's $3.00 plus tax spent in one week. Multiplied by 52 weeks, that's $156 dollars in one year. By 1998 standards, that represents approximately 10 CDs, 13 trips to a movie for a happy couple, or 2 exceptionally good seats at a NASCAR race in Charlotte (I had to throw in one of my interests). If asked which I would rather have, the answer seems clear enough. I would much rather have a CD playing timely tunes in my living room while my daughter and I dance (which is quite a sight) than a few gulps of a giant soft drink.

Why do we purchase them then? Of course, it's convenient. Just as it's convenient not to really concentrate on working toward our goals on a daily basis. It's the easy way out. If, however, we look at the cost of taking the easy way out over a long period of time, the scenario begins to change. Lost opportunity (time, educational opportunities, financial resources) can never be recovered. Ever tried recycling plastic soda bottles? A neighbor once had a dump truck almost full of them. He got $5.00. Yes, recycling is good for the environment, but not regularly purchasing them in the first place would have been an even smarter choice. As a teacher, I used to get so angry with students who whined about paying $3.00 for this field trip or $2.00 for that project. "I don't have the money, Mr. Loflin, I'm broke." A day or two later I would see them walking with a 1 liter "Big Slam" Mountain Dew and respond, "I thought you were broke?" Their reply, "Mr. Loflin, I had to have my drink." Instant gratification poster child.

Please don't get me wrong. I sometimes purchase those infamous bottles of carbonated concoctions myself when travelling on a long trip. Buying them on a regular basis, however, is costly, just as wasting our resources of education, energy, and opportunity is costly over the long haul. Putting off advancing a degree, restoring a strained relationship, or simply reading more books may seem harmless now.

Watch, however, as we struggle to maintain job security. Watch as the strain in the relationship brings destruction to our family units. Those few moments of convenience just do not seem as important now.

Oh, if you want a solution to the mountain of polypropylene (plastic) and spent cash, see the money management chapter.

Goals with VALUE

Acronyms are all the rage today, especially in business and education. TQM, VOCATS, PDQ, PMA, GED and IEP are just a few. They have become so prevalent that one educator said, "All these programs with acronyms are so confusing...they are as clear to me as M.U.D." (It was funnier when the teacher said it to a college professor who said they had not heard of that program.) That said, I just could not miss an opportunity to be in vogue and give you an acronym of my own as it relates to goals. To reach these goals more successfully, they should be:

V	**Value Oriented**
A	**Active**
L	**Layered**
U	**Unique**
E	**Explainable**

V   Value Oriented

When I talk with young people, I have to smile as I listen to their goals and dreams. It is very refreshing to hear of plans unbridled by age, circumstances, or the negative influences of others. One question I sometimes inject into the conversation is "Why have you set that goal?" Unfortunately, the youthful smile will sometimes turn to a melancholy grin as the young person ponders their response. Next will come comments like, "My mom thought this career would..." or "I have a friend who is also a ..." or "You make good money at..." or "My boyfriend/girlfriend and I are getting married and..." The list goes on and on.

The next group, those who have completed their education (high school or college) and are settling down, have their own set of goals. Often, the reasons are material in nature. To get a house with a certain set of amenities, to reach a certain pinnacle of success in a job, to achieve a specific level financially, or to provide in a particular way for their family. More abstract goals, if expressed (they can be postponed until later, they say), talk of a desire to make their life count for something. I normally don't ask these individuals why. Their goals speak for themselves as reflections of a society that screams "you can have it all."

Mature adults (some are 15, others are 95), on the other hand, are a little different. As they discuss their goals (if they do...many will not because stating their goals will create a need for commitment to reach them) you can hear the why in their words. Goals now have become a reflection of who they are, an outward statement of an inward being. Goals increasingly originate from beliefs or values they hold and want expressed in their actions. It is this group that has learned the strength of Value-oriented goals.

To begin setting goals that are an outgrowth of your values, you may want to refer back to the chapter on values to "find yourself." For a quick start, try this scenario:

Having reached the age of 70, you are chosen to speak to a group of young people about being successful. They ask for a written introduction, and you hand them a resume'. It does not include your educational background, address, awards, or professional achievements. In other words, it talks about who you are as a person. What will it say?

Having done that, move on to the next step, creating a laundry list. Below your unusual resume', list the things you need to do in order to be the person you described in the resume'. Don't attach times, specifics, or any restraining information. Just list them! Yes, class, I know this is painful, but remember, "No pain, no gain." It's uncomfortable to write things that may require us to change the way we operate on a daily basis. Remember, though;

"As the want gets stronger, the how gets easier."

Seem like proverbial pie in the sky? Let's look at one of my examples. In my unusual resume' I would list, "He is a good father." There are literally hundreds of things that I could list to try and be a good father, but here are a few:

- Be a role model for her
- Spend quality and quantity time with her
- Provide for her needs: Physical, mental, spiritual, financial

After reviewing this short list, I see all kinds of implications about my career and marriage as well as the importance of personal example. If I take into consideration all my values before setting any goal, I have a concrete reason to pursue the goal with all my strength and abilities, because it reflects who I am as a person.

Easy? No. I have to remind myself often that life is a triathlon, not a sprint. Life is not a series of "quick" decisions but rather a long procession of hills and valleys, land and water, swimming, running and biking. To complete the race more successfully, I must pace myself. Too much energy expended in one area will hurt me in another. The pace is set by our values. They help us see the finish line instead of limiting us to the next curve, hill, or obstacle in our path.

A   Active

We have already discussed at great length our failure to see the imminent need to pursue our goals every day. Regardless of the nature of the goal, something can almost always be done to progress toward its achievement. You, being the devil's advocate, are busily trying to think of a goal that has no daily demands. In response to your negative attitude (shame on you), here are some examples:

- High school student preparing for college - maintain grades daily
- Trying to read 5 novels this year - Use 30 minutes wasted in front of the TV
- Saving for a new item of clothing - stay away from the soda machine (you knew that was coming)

- Looking for a better career? - Read want ads and magazines, sharpen interview skills
- Trying to be a better spouse - Take 2 minutes and do something for them (i.e. note, hold their hand, extra hug, buy their favorite candy)

Again, the possibilities are endless. The key is keeping the goal in our conscious mind each day so that it guides our thoughts and actions, instead of being led by emotion, circumstances, or merely the influence of other people.

L   Layered or Lumped Together
     Pizza is one of my favorite foods. I do believe I could eat good, hot, thick-crust pizza until I literally exploded. Having partaken of pizza all across the United States, I am still partial to the basic order of crust, tomato paste, and toppings. Any other way just does not appeal to me, *unless* it is an imploded pizza (commonly referred to as stromboli). If you ever invite me to speak to your organization and want to really make my day, take me to an Italian restaurant that serves good stromboli. Wait a minute, you say. There is a world of difference between a pizza and stromboli. One has a precise order, whereas the other can be completed as desired once the crust is in place. Okay, you got me. To be honest, however, my taste buds do not care.
     Our goals are sometimes like pizza and other times like stromboli. Certain goals, like acquiring a college education or higher degree, have definite layers. One must enroll, attend and pass classes, and graduate. Others, however, do not have a precise order. Being a good father can take any number of forms in almost any order once the child enters this world. One can "lump" such activities together.
     An acquaintance of mine was constantly telling me about his desire to drive a road tractor (tractor-trailer rig). His eyes sparkled as he recalled memories of recent part time experiences (he had another full time job). Wanting to be helpful, I asked about the necessary steps to get him to his goal. Dejected, he would talk despairingly about the cost of a truck. When asked about a partnership, he would change the subject. When asked about buying one now and paying it off while working his current job, he talked about the horrors of having someone else drive his truck. Needless to say, he still does not have a road

tractor. He was just not willing to look at the layers necessary to make his dream a reality. Even something small like saving a few dollars or finding someone who could provide his financial backing would be a place to start. He wanted to lump all that together, however, making everything happen at once, and it just could not happen with this type of goal (unless he won the lottery).

U   Unique

My wife and I live in a three-bedroom brick home built in the 1970's. Very little renovations had taken place when we bought it in 1993. Yes, the carpet was that wonderful orange/brown mingle, the bathroom wallpaper a hideous green and brown (with bunny rabbits on it), and the kitchen small, but by far the most annoying part of our new pad was the overhead lighting...or lack thereof. With the exception of the kitchen, foyer, and one end of the living room, there were *no* overhead lights. Each room had a wonderful outlet controlled by a switch that activated a lamp or whatever was plugged into it. When inquiring of those who were around when the house was built, they replied, "Well, it was just the way many houses were built during that time." Upon moving in, our first major expenditure was to install overhead lighting in all the rooms. We now proudly have all rooms well lit (which is a bummer because you can see the dust and clutter and soon realize that maybe the original owners were onto something).

Do our goals reflect who we want to be, or are they simply built the way others around us built theirs? Just like the house Lisa and I bought, we find ourselves having to "remodel" our goals because they were patterned after someone else's talents and abilities. Why not build them the way "we" want them the first time?

Watch pointing that finger solely at young people! Yes, young people are more susceptible to the influences of friends and society as they plan their lives, but we "more experienced" people may be guilty of cookie cutter goals as well. Trying to accumulate material things like our peers or achieve levels of professional greatness or social acceptance are frequent mistakes made by those of any age. Having achieved it all, we look around saying, "Is this it?" Meanwhile, we leave the deeper dreams and goals because we were afraid to be different.

Jerry Richardson may not be a household name in your part of the country. His rise to greatness, however, symbolizes to me someone who had a goal that was unique. In the late 1960's Jerry Richardson had just completed his first year with the Baltimore Colts and had an outstanding season. In his second year there was a contract dispute. Jerry wanted $10,000 while the Colts only offered him $9750 (oh, for the good ol' days). He responded to the dispute with "I am going home to sell hamburgers." Really, he did. His belief was that people would buy hamburgers prepared quickly and served hot. Although his friends pleaded with him to reconsider, he refused and went home. In the first few years he worked seven days a week, sharing a car with another man, selling hamburgers for 15 cents each. Today, Jerry Richardson is the owner of the 4th largest retail food service organization in the world. His list of restaurants and franchises includes Quincy's, Dennys and Hardees, along with other more regional ones. He is a common name in North Carolina because he is also the owner of the Carolina Panthers NFL Team. Not bad for someone who had a unique goal and stuck to it.

E   Explainable

Sounds simple enough, being able to express our heartfelt dreams and goals to others. You would be amazed, however, to know how many people cannot tell you in words what it is they hope to achieve in life. They have an idea, but have never been prodded to explain it to someone else. It is in this sharing, however, that a number of things happen. First, it crystallizes the plan, even when the other person remains silent. Ever said something in such a way that it makes no sense? My wife says I do it often. In fact, we all have thoughts or comments that may be confusing to someone else. There are stories I use in some of my programs that were real duds when I first used them. Over time, though, I have refined and honed them to create a story with a clear (er) point. The same is true of our thoughts. The more they are brought to the surface by sharing, the more we can analyze and adjust them to better understand them.

Secondly, explaining your goal to others creates an air of expectancy and commitment. Once you share it with someone, you become obliged to do something about it. They will probably not berate you if you fail to reach it, but they will expect to see you working towards it. Additionally, if others know of your intentions, it creates a desire within you to achieve it because you do not want to appear a failure to others or diminish their confidence in your abilities.

Summing It Up

I close with two examples of goals from my own life. One is a layered goal (with intermediate steps), while the other is one in which the elements are lumped together.

Lumped Together
Value: *I am a good father.*
Goals: I spend quality and quantity time with my child each week.
I read at least one book to Alex each day.
I arise by 6:00 AM each day to meet some of my profes
sional and personal responsibilities. (i.e. to give me the
opportunity to be with her during breakfast)
I evaluate my actions and words to insure they set the proper
example for her to follow.

Layered (or Levels)
Value: I am a financially successful individual.
Long Range Goal: By June 1998 my wife leaves full time employ-ment. (to be a full time mom, assist with H.O.P.E., Inc., pursue her own hobbies/interests)

Intermediate Goal: By August, 1997, I am booking at least one pro-gram per week.

Short Range Goal: By December, 1996, I am mailing and/or contact-ing at least 4000 potential clients.
Daily Goals:
• Get up early to input addresses/information into computer.
• Adequately prepare for upcoming programs so that other individuals will have the desire to choose me for one of their future conferences or meetings.

• When a request for information is made, promotional packet will be in the mail in 24 hours or less.

• Maintain contact with past clients to let them know about new workshops or keynotes.

How am I doing? At this point Alex does not seem to have any maladjusted tendencies and has developed into a wonderful little girl (the influence of her mother no doubt). As for the business and Lisa being at home, it happened in July, 1997. I wish you could have seen us celebrating that day. I had purchased a hammock for her and put it up in the back yard. Next to it was a six pack of her favorite beverage, *Yoo Hoo* (a chocolate drink... you were expecting something else?). At the carport was a huge banner that read, "Welcome home, we love you!" Along the road approaching our house was a series of signs that read: *Roses Are Red, Fudge Ripple comes in a swirl, Lisa is now home, to be with her little girl.*

When she drove up at 12:00 noon, Alex and I were jumping up and down and screaming, "Welcome home!" We immediately escorted her to the hammock and served a sandwich lunch followed by the chocolate nectar of *Yoo Hoos* (you might be a redneck if...). I wish you could have seen the smile on her face.

Why do I share that strange personal story? Simply because it is so easy to lose sight of the rewards of achieving a goal. Other people will try to tear us down, circumstances seem to work against us, and often we just get worn out in the process. If we set goals that have VALUE, however, and work to reach those goals, the end results are often more rewarding than we ever imagined. Even if the goal is not fully met, we have the satisfaction of a clear conscience that is not asking, "What if?"

H

Humor

Know a good joke? Let me rephrase that: Do you know a good *clean* joke? Don't feel bad, most people are in your same shoes. It is increasingly scary to me, at the droves of individuals who cannot tell a clean joke. Instead, they resort to ones that involve grossly degrading another race, gender, or ethnic group. They shrug it off by saying, "It was only a joke." Okay, let me take a hammer and bean you on the side of your head (your friends might think it was funny watching you stagger around). "It was only a joke," I would say. Funny now? That's the same way others feel emotionally or mentally after a joke that diminishes who they are as a person. Not to appear too saintly, I have been there as well. More than once in high school or college I shared a joke that would not be appropriate in certain circles. I then noticed that my friends would tell me jokes in return later that had the same negative tones. If we were together long enough, someone in the group would comment on the validity of the joke, and that would go places no one needed to be. We will talk more about image in the next chapter, so let's go to Humorville for the remainder of this one.

On the following pages are a compilation of one liners and jokes I find amusing (notice I do not make the wholesale assumption that they *are* funny or that you will find them so) and clean. Some people will, no doubt, find something offensive in them, and if you do, please accept my apologies. As my good friend Patrick Grady says, "I did not come here to make you mad, I came here to make you laugh and to think." Many of them can be adapted to fit your needs, whether you are simply in a conversation with friends or giving a presentation and need a light moment. Yes, you will have heard some of these jokes before, but I have found that jokes are like aluminum cans...they get recycled more now than ever.

One Liners
- Lottery: Tax on people who are bad at math.
- The early bird gets the worm, but the second mouse gets the cheese.
- When everything is coming your way, you are in the wrong lane.
- I could not repair your brakes, so I made your horn louder.
- All those who believe in psychokinesis, raise my hand.
- If it's tourist season, why can't we shoot them?
- Ever stop to think, and forget to start again?

Strange Questions
- Why do you need a driver's license to buy liquor when you cannot drink and drive?
- Why are there flotation devices under plane seats instead of parachutes?
- If our nose runs and feet smell, were we built upside down?
- If one synchronized swimmer drowns, do the rest have to drown too?
- If you're in a car going the speed of light, what would happen if you turned your headlights on?
- What did people go back to before there were drawing boards?
- If olive oil is made from olives, what is baby oil made from?
- Why do they sterilize needles used for lethal injection?
- How can there be "Self-help"groups?
- Why isn't there mouse-flavored cat food?

Bumper Stickers
- The kids drive me crazy, and I drive them everywhere.
- Horn broken - watch for finger.
- Why am I the only person on earth who knows how to drive?!
- Do not steal. The government does not like the competition.

- Women who seek to be equal to men lack ambition.
- Will Rogers never met a lawyer.
- There's one in every crowd, and they always find me.
- Crime would not pay if the government ran it.
- I don't care who you are, what your other car is, where you would rather be, or who your kid is.
- Give blood - Play hockey.

Miscellaneous jokes

Customer: Waiter, this food is not fit for a pig.
Waiter: I will take it back, sir, and bring you some that is.

Customer: Do I have to wait here until I die of starvation?
Waiter: No sir, we close at six o'clock.

Customer: Call the manager. I can't eat this stuff!
Waiter: It's no use, sir, he can't eat it either.

Ricky: "My great grandfather came to Canada seeking freedom.
Eddie: Did he find it?
Ricky: No. My great grandmother came over on the very next boat."

If you have trouble getting your children's attention, just sit down and look comfortable.

A boy called the doctor. "Doctor, doctor, come quick, my younger brother has swallowed my pen!" The doctor said, "I will be right over! What are you doing in the meantime?
The boy replied, "Using a pencil."

Two guys walked down the street. Suddenly, one of them kneeled down and picked up a small mirror. He looked at it and said, "Hey, I think I know this man! "Let me see that," his friend said as he grabbed the mirror. "Of course you know this guy! It's me, stupid!"

Boy: Help! My brother thinks he's a chicken!
Doctor: Oh my! How long has he been this way?
Boy: Two years.
Doctor: Why on earth did you wait two years to get help?
Boy: We needed the eggs.

A woman walked up to the manager of a department store. "Are you hiring any help?" she asked. "No" the manager replied. "We have all the staff we need."
"Then would you mind getting someone to wait on me?" the woman asked.

"Dad, can you write in the dark?" the little boy asked.
"Sure, son. When I was in college, I had to do it often because my roommate was a late sleeper."
"Good," the little boy replied, "turn off the lights and sign my report card."

Because of a dense fog, a Mississippi steamboat had to stop at the mouth of a river. A woman passenger demanded to know the cause of the delay. "I cannot see up the river," the captain replied. "Fog is too thick." "But I can see the stars overhead," the woman pointed out. "Yes," the captain growled, "But unless the boilers explode, we're not going that way!"

A man was in his back yard when he glanced next door and saw his neighbor digging a hole. Inquiring his friend, he was told, "My canary died and I am burying it." "Oh, I'm sorry to hear that," said the first neighbor, "but isn't that a pretty big hole for your little canary?" "Well, it's inside your darn cat!" came the reply.

"What am I supposed to do?" a young man asked. "Every woman I bring home to meet my parents, my mother does not like." "Oh, that's easy," his friend replied. "All you have to do is find someone who is just like your mother." "I already tried that!" the young man cried. "My father didn't like her!"

A 911 operator received a call from a clearly intoxicated caller. "Thieves got into my car!" the man said. "They took the steering wheel, foot pedals, and the whole dashboard!" The operator said they would send someone to investigate, and a few minutes later the phone rang again. "Never mind," the same voice said, "I moved into the front seat and there it all was."

One friend to another:
"My girlfriend got mad when I used the word garbage."
"That's not such a bad word."
"Yeah, and to me that's what her dinner tasted like!"

Judge to defendant: "Have you anything to offer this court before sentence is passed on you?"
Defendant: "No, your honor. My lawyer took my last dollar."

Emerging from the chiropractor's treatment room, a young man said aloud in the crowded waiting room, "I feel like a new man!" "I do, too," a middle aged woman responded, "but I'll probably go home with the same old one."

What is the difference between a peeping Tom and someone who's just gotten out of the shower? One is rude and nosy while the other is nude and rosy.

A lawyer died suddenly at age 45. He got to the gates of Heaven, and the angel standing there said, "We have been waiting a long time for you." "What do you mean?" he replied. " I am only 45, in the prime of my life. Why did I have to die now?" "45? You are not 45 sir, you are 102," the angel replied. "Wait a minute. If you think I am 102, then you have the wrong guy. I am only 45. I can show you my birth certificate." "Hold on. Let me go check," said the angel, and he disappeared inside. After a few minutes the angel returned. "Sorry, but by our records you are 102. I checked all the hours you have billed your clients, and you *have* to be 102."

A policeman pulled a woman over after she had been driving the wrong way on a one-way street. He said, "Do you know where you were going?" She replied, "No, but wherever it is, it must be bad because all the people were leaving."

"Sam, why don't you play golf with Joe anymore?" Sam's wife asked. "Would you play golf with someone who moved the ball with his foot when you were not watching?" Sam replied. "Well, no," admitted his wife. "And neither will Ted," replied Sam.

A man with two red ears went to his doctor. The doctor asked him what happened to his ears, and he answered, "I was ironing a shirt and the phone rang - but instead of picking up the phone I accidentally picked up the iron and stuck it to my ear." "Oh, dear!" the doctor exclaimed. "But...what happened to your other ear?" The man replied, "Whoever it was called back."

Johnny and his classmates had just finished a tour of the local fire station. Before the students left, the fire chief asked each a question. He asked Johnny, "What do you do if your clothes catch on fire?" Johnny replied, "I do not put them on."

A woman came home and shouted to her husband, "Honey! Pack your bags! I won the lottery!" "Should I pack for warm or cold weather?" asked her husband. "It really doesn't matter, just as long as you're out of here in an hour!" she replied.

Marie: I just burned a hundred dollar bill.
Jane: Wow! You must be rich!
Marie: Not really. The bill was from my dentist!

A Sunday school teacher, lacking in subject matter, was discussing with her class how Noah might have spent his time on the ark. A girl's answer was, "Maybe he went fishing." A boy countered with, "With only two worms?"

A man counseled his son that if he wanted to live a long life, the secret was to sprinkle a little gunpowder on his cereal every morning. The son did this religiously, and he lived to the age of 93. When he died, he left 14 children, 28 grand-children, 35 great-grandchildren, and a 15 foot hole in the wall of the crematorium.

Sign on a company bulletin board: "This firm requires no physical fitness programs. Everyone gets enough exercise jumping to conclusions, running down management, flying off the handle, beating dead horses, stabbing fellow employees in the back, dodging responsibility, and pushing their luck."

An artist asked the gallery owner if anyone had shown interest in his paintings. "I have good news and bad news," she said. "The good news is that some guy inquired if your paintings would appreciate in value after you died. When I told him they would, he bought all 15 of your paintings." "And the bad news?" asked the artist. "The guy was your doctor."

A man goes to the hospital to have an operation on his hand. He asks, "Doctor, will I be able to play the piano after the operation?" "But of course," replies the doctor. "Wow! Great! I couldn't play it before."

A nurse was listening while a doctor was yelling, "Typhoid! Tetanus! Measles!" The nurse asked another nurse, "Why is he doing that?" The other nurse replied, "Oh, he just likes to call the shots around here."

A farmer and his wife went to a fair. The farmer was fascinated by the airplanes and asked a pilot how much a ride would cost. "$10 for 3 minutes," replied the pilot. "That's too much," said the farmer. The pilot thought for a moment and then said, 'I will make you a deal. If you and your wife ride for 3 minutes without uttering a sound, the ride will be free. But if you make a sound, you have to pay the $10." The farmer and his wife agreed and went for a wild ride. After they land, the pilot said to the farmer, "I want to congratulate you for not making a sound. You were a brave man." "Maybe so," said the farmer, "but I gotta tell ya, I almost screamed when my wife fell out."

Two men were robbing a hotel. The first one said, "I hear sirens! Jump!" The second one said, "But we are on the 13th floor!" The first one screamed back, "This is no time to be superstitious."

Late one night, a burglar broke into a house that he thought was empty. He tiptoed through the living room, but suddenly he froze in his tracks when he heard a loud voice say, "Jesus is watching you!" Silence returned to the house, so the burglar crept forward. "Jesus is watching you!" the voice boomed again. The frightened burglar stopped dead. Frantically, he looked all around. In a dark corner, he spotted a bird cage, and in the cage was a parrot. He asked the parrot, "Was that you who said Jesus is watching me?" "Yes," replied the parrot. The burglar breathed a sigh of relief, then he asked the parrot, "What is your name?" "Clarence," said the bird. "That is a ridiculous name for a parrot," sneered the burglar. "What idiot named you Clarence?" The parrot said, "The same idiot who named the Doberman Jesus."

A boss did not come into work one day. He called early that morning and told his secretary he was having vision problems. When she asked what was wrong, he replied, "I just cannot see myself coming to work today."

An obviously intoxicated man flopped on a subway seat next to a priest. The man's clothes were stained, his face was plastered with lipstick, and a bottle of whiskey was hanging out of his coat pocket. He opened his newspaper and began reading. After a few minutes the disheveled guy turned to the priest and asked, "Father, what causes arthritis?" "Mister, it is caused by loose living, being with prostitutes, too much alcohol, and a contempt for your fellow man." "Well, I'll be," the drunk muttered, returning to his paper. The priest, thinking about his harsh tone, nudged the man and apologized. "I am very sorry, I did not mean to be so violent. How long have you had arthritis?" "Oh, I don't have it, Father. I was just reading here that the Pope does."

Lisa: If you have two dollars, and you ask your father for four dollars, how much will you have?
Renee: Two dollars.
Lisa: You don't know your math.
Renee: You don't know my father!

An inmate was aware that all prison mail passes through censors. When he got a letter from his wife asking, "Honey, when do I plant potatoes in the family garden?" he wrote back: "Do not, under any circumstances, dig up our old garden spot. That is where I buried all my guns." Within days his wife wrote back, "Six investigators came to the house. They dug up every square inch of the our garden." She got his answer by return mail, "Now is the time to plant potatoes."

A man was giving a speech at his lodge meeting. He got a bit carried away and talked for two hours. Finally, he realized what he had done and said, "I'm sorry I talked so long. I left my watch at home." A voice from the back of the room replied, "There's a calendar behind you!"

A sergeant was instructing a new paratrooper before his first jump. "Count to 10 and pull the first rip cord. If that does not work, pull the second rip cord for the auxiliary chute. After you land, a truck will pick you up." The paratrooper jumped, counted to ten and pulled the first cord. Nothing happened. He pulled the second cord... and nothing happened. He then said to himself, "I bet the truck won't be there either!"

Prosecutor: Did you kill the victim?
Defendant: No, I certainly did not!
Prosecutor: Are you aware of the penalties for perjury?
Defendant: Yes, I am and they are a heck of a lot better than the penalty for murder.

A man was passing a country estate and saw a sign on the gate. It read: "Please ring bell for the caretaker." He rang the bell and an old man appeared. "Are you the caretaker?" the man asked. "Yes, I am," replied the old man. "what do you want?" "I would just like to know why you can't ring the bell."

Preacher: The people in this church are so thoughtful. They are dedicating a plaque to those who have died in the service.
Church Member: Which service-Morning or Evening?

After dinner one evening, a rancher's wife was entertaining their house guest by playing the piano. At one point she turned to the visitor and said, "I understand you love music." "Yes," murmured the guest politely. "But never you mind. Keep right on playing."

A father took his young daughter to the grocery store with him. In addition to the healthful items on the mother's list, they returned with a box of sugar-rich cookies. Noticing his wife's glare, the husband said, 'This box of cookies has one-third fewer calories than usual." "Why is that?" she asked. "We ate a third of the cookies on the way home," he replied.

A guy dies suddenly without writing a will. The distressed widow goes to a lawyer and explains the problem. The lawyer asks, "Did your husband say anything to you before he died?" She replied, "Yes, he said, 'Mary, you can not hit the broad side of a barn with that thing, so put it down.'"

A lady driving on Highway 64 was racing along when a policeman stopped her. "Madam, why were you going so fast?" "Well," the lady replied, "I saw the sign back there that said '64', and I was just going the speed limit." The patrolman sighed. "It's a good thing I caught you before you got to Interstate 95."

Husband: Let's go out and have some fun tonight.
Wife: Okay, but if you get home before I do, leave the hallway light on.

Two truck drivers were driving along a highway late one night when they approached a tunnel that had a sign saying, "CLEARANCE 3.1 METERS." The first driver says, "Okay, we will have to turn the truck around `cause it is 4 meters high," and the second replied, "Look. It's the middle of the night, and no cops are around. I say we go for it!"

A criminal is on the electric chair and starts to get the hiccups while the warden prepares to pull the switch. The warden asks, "Do you have any last requests?" The criminal replies, "(hic) Yeah... (hic) could you please do (hic) could you please do something to scare me?"

Husband: I have a problem.
Marriage Counselor: What is the problem?
Husband: My wife and I cannot agree on our vacation.
Marriage Counselor: That doesn't sound so bad.
Husband: No, you don't understand. I want to go to Bermuda, and she wants to go with me.

Knowing her husband's habit of sampling everything she baked, a woman left a note on a dozen cookies reading, "Counted-one dozen." When she returned, two cookies were missing and a second note read, "Think metric."

Staking out a notoriously rowdy bar for possible drunk drivers, a cop watched from his squad car as a fellow stumbled out the door, tripped on the curb, and tried five cars before opening the door to his own and falling asleep on the front seat. One by one, the drivers of the other cars drove off. Finally, the sleeper woke up, started his car and began to leave. The cop pulled him over and administered a Breathalyzer test. When the results showed a 0.0 blood-alcohol level, the puzzled policeman asked him how that has possible. "Easy," was the reply. "Tonight was my turn to be the decoy."

At a party a woman was talking to a doctor. "What kind of doctor are you?" she asked. "A Naval Surgeon," he replied. "My, how you doctors specialize," she said.

I

Image

A t a recent youth conference, one of the adult chaperones walked up to me and said, "Are you our speaker for tonight?" "Yes, I am," I replied enthusiastically. His response was, "Do you know how many professional speakers it takes to replace a light bulb?" Getting this strange feeling that I was about to be dumped on, I said, "Uh...no. How many does it take?" "None," came his jovial snarl, "they think the world revolves around them so they just hold it up, and it replaces itself." My reply was, "After this weekend is over you tell me if you have seen any of those tendencies in me. I'm not perfect, but I don't intend to resemble that remark."

Talking with another speaker who had been in the presence of this man, he told me that he had been slapped with the same provocative punch line. Apparently, that was an image perpetuated by the speakers this individual had heard in the past. Of course, I wanted to scream, "I am not like that!" but simply saying it would be like putting low-calorie maple syrup on pancakes: It would just not have the same impact (on my taste buds in this instance). Something would have to be done to correct this man's image of a professional speaker.

Image. It has become a paradox in our society. On the one hand we are told to express ourselves like never before. Clothing styles, cars, foods, and even our choice of chewing gum are all part of our identity to others. On the other hand, we cry "foul" because we want others to mold their opinions of us by who we are on the *inside*, personality, skills, and achievements. Where is the medium (whether happy or not) whereby we can adequately project who we are as a person and not have people create some immediate wrong conceptions about who we are professionally and/or personally?

Youth groups are among the most challenging to me when trying to address the concept of image. In many of my presentations to schools, I use a variety of ways to help young people understand that whom and what they hang around with speaks much more about them than people will ever take the time to actually learn about them. "That's not fair," they often reply. "Would you ask someone out who constantly had body odor?" I ask. "Why of course not. That's such a turn off." "But what if they are a really neat person on the inside?" comes my response. "It doesn't matter," they say, "I could never get past the smell." You know the rest of the story. In a perfect world, it would be great if people would ask us about our beliefs, values, and thoughts on certain issues before molding their opinions of us. We live in a fast-food world, however, where we choose the combo meal because it takes less time to think about (and is cheaper per item), and we can move on to something else. It may not be what we actually wanted (a sit down meal at a restaurant), but it eases the hunger. People want to determine quickly if they want to be a part of our life (ordering) so they can get on with other stuff in life. The image we project is like the menu. What do people quickly see (or hear) that they like about us?

A disclaimer: I do not begin to see myself as a professional image consultant. Many of you who will read this book will have seen me at a conference or meeting and will immediately ponder, "What do I remember about Jones?" Hopefully, the memories will be positive ones. I am not, however, a guru. More than once my internal me has been misinterpreted because of something my external me said or did. This chapter merely offers some advice based on my personal experiences and those with other individuals and organizations. Make it fit for your situation and/or organization to receive the maximum benefit.

Your Clothes

What do your clothes say about you? My pants frequently say, "How do you plan to stretch the waist today?" Seriously, though, do your clothes fit the occasion? No doubt you have laughed at actors or performers who show up at formal Hollywood gatherings wearing something completely inappropriate for the occasion. When you become famous for much more than your way of dress, that may be okay. For us commoners, however, a different approach may be necessary if we want to project a particular image and gain desired results.

One of my ongoing studies at the Center for Practical Stuff (H.O.P.E. Inc.) is to examine the relationship between dress and the customer service I receive. You already know the answer from watching TV talk shows (and hearing people whine about it not being fair), but have you ever personally experienced how your image affects the customer service you receive? While staying in motels, inns, and conference centers I have experienced everything from noisy neighbors to no water (really) to no TV sound (not a big deal). I do complain when necessary and try to be cordial and offer solutions when possible. Often, I will personally go to the front desk instead of talking on the phone, since a degree of urgency is brought to the situation when "He's here."

The day manager usually comes in around 8:00 AM, so I try to go to the desk when I am sure they are on duty. Sometimes I wear my jeans, the shirt I slept in, and my glasses, without combing my hair. Other times I go ahead and dress in my suit before approaching the desk. At a stay in Tennessee a few years ago, I had a terrible experience. The hotel (an upscale chain) was not as it should have been. The rooms were not properly cleaned, people were being noisy in the hall all through the evening and night, and we had trouble getting clean towels after a trip to the pool. I went to the desk (after calling a couple of times) dressed in my shorts and T-shirt and complained to the manager on duty. He assured me he would take care of it. I asked about being moved, but he said that the hotel was full. Being so late in the night, I knew there was nothing that could be done since many of the hotels were already full. What really ticked me off, however, was the demeaning nature of his words to me and my wife. The next morning, I arose and dressed for the day in my suit. Upon loading the van, I went to the desk to check out. The front desk clerk said, "Good morning, how was your stay?" "Okay, I guess," was my reply. She immediately took my bill and stepped to the back office. She returned with Mr. Rude himself (the manager from the night before), and he pertly replied, "Mr. Loflin, was there a problem last night?" Instead of screaming, I politely opened my planner and listed all the problems from the night before. He expressed his sincere regret with the way things had gone and asked about making things right. I received 20% off my hotel room and the assurance that if I would stay my second night (I had planned to be there 2 nights) everything would be in order. I then dropped the bomb- "Why didn't you tell me all this last night?" "I don't understand," he replied. "Why didn't you offer me all these things when I came up here yesterday?" was my comment. I refreshed his memory about me dressed in my other clothes, then Lisa and I left the hotel. Whether we like to admit it or not, our clothes do have an instantaneous impact on how people perceive us.

In my early days in public speaking, money was tight. With only one full-time income and a baby on the way, we carefully watched every dime. One area I refused (well, my wife actually helped me refuse) to skimp on, however, was my clothes. Granted, I did not like spending large amounts on suits, shirts, and shoes, but who wants to see a "professional" speaker who does not look professional? Our clothes (including our shoes) do tell the story.

What to Wear

Here are some thoughts that seem to work well for others as well as me when attempting to decide what to wear to look professional.

Determine what others will be wearing. If you are representing your organization and there is a standard dress (color scheme, type of suit, etc.) for your company, then that would be in order. If you are in a host or leadership capacity, dress as well as or one step above the other participants. If everyone else is in shorts and T-shirts, wear a collared shirt and dress shorts. If everyone else is in dress slacks (or similar mode for ladies), a coat and tie (casual business suit for ladies) may be appropriate. You get the picture. Dressing one step above the others does not mean you are trying to make others feel inferior, it simply says, "I take my role as a leader in this situation seriously." I cannot begin to recall the number of times people have approached me at meetings with questions about location of restrooms, meeting times, or other needs because they perceived that I was in charge from my clothing. If you are simply a participant in the activity, dress in accordance with the other members of the group. If not told, ask about expected dress for the occasion... don't guess. A few years ago I was asked to speak to a group of students at a banquet. Banquet... dress up, right? So I donned my formal suit (they will be in professional dress) and arrived at the meeting to find 180 high school students in T-shirts and shorts. Even the adults at the banquet were similarly dressed. I quickly shed the tie and coat but wished I could have found a pair of khakis (my wife says I own 50 pair) and a polo shirt. Ask, Ask, Ask.

Organizational Standard of Dress

If you really want to have a verbal field day with a group of people, try to create a standard of dress for your organization. Many youth organizations have an official dress (normally consisting of a certain type of blazer and color coordination of slacks, skirts, and shirts/blouses) that is worn when officially representing an organization. Beyond that, however, there are usually very few standards set up for what is appropriate at other times. I find that scary. In my opinion, the image projected by the members of an organization at the unofficial times is the one most often seen by others.

While attending one youth conference, I was greatly impressed to learn that they have a standard of dress at all times. From competing in contests to just walking around the hotel, minimum guidelines suggested what was okay to wear. "Jones, you're going overboard here," you say. Young people might dress inappropriately, but adults know how to project a professional image with their clothes. Oh, really? Go to a youth conference and watch some of the adults serving as chaperones or advisors. Then it will not be so difficult for you to perceive the need for *everyone* to seriously examine their clothing choices.

When speaking at a conference in the morning, I frequently arrive the evening before to avoid rushing in at the last minute or having a flight cancelled. Some groups will have a president's reception or social time where any members who wish can come and talk with other members and catch up on stuff. It has become something of a game for me to attend these functions and try to pick out the board of directors and/or key people in the group. The organizations that seem to have their act together usually (there are exceptions) have officers who are dressed very professionally with a minimum number wearing something that whispers, "Where is the local night club?" They may dress that way later or when they are back home, but they have learned the vital lesson that an organization is judged heavily by the professionalism of the most noticeable and/or prominent members of the organization.

As a meeting facilitator some time ago, I had the job of assisting teams of youth organization officers with developing a code of conduct for the officers of their individual organizations. The team members that struggled the most were the ones evaluating proper dress. No matter what direction I tried to steer them, they just sat around and whined about people's clothes being an expression of their individuality. At one point I even said, "Are there clothing styles that would inhibit your function as an officer?" "No," was their reply. I was subtly trying to refer to those short skirts that are once again prominent in our culture. These officers would be working with high school and middle school students, performing activities that would require them to reach, stoop, and be free to move around. Having been unintentionally flashed by more than one young lady forgetting what she was wearing, I wanted them to see how easily their choice of clothing could be a distraction and diminish their level of professionalism. In other words, drawing attention to themselves instead of their organization. No takers here. Not wanting to be labeled as an old fogey, I went in another direction. I came up with a scenario. I said, "What if you were the only member of your organization those people would ever see? How would that affect the way you dress?" Apparently, it struck a nerve. It was difficult for them to see the importance of adjusting their clothing styles based on individual preferences, but it became easier once they saw it in the context of being a representative of their organization.

My wife Lisa taught me a great deal about this as well. She travels with me, whenever possible, to my programs. That was one of our goals when we started this business, and our experiences have been wonderful. It used to irritate me to see Lisa struggle over what to wear for a function. Her role would frequently be to videotape the program, so my thought was "What does it matter as long as she is clothed? They will be watching me." That sounds egotistical, but you get the point. Finally, she said, "Jones, people see me around the hotel with you. They see us walk in together and talking with each other. More than once people have approached me and asked me questions about your programs or about H.O.P.E. I need to look my best since they may never approach you." What a brilliant thought. Wish I'd thought of it. We have to approach our clothing styles from much the same manner in professional situations, even when not in official capacities. Remember, you may be the only _____ (your organization) member someone ever sees, and they may see you by the pool, in the elevator, or in a place you never imagined.

Closely connected to the clothing style is the accessories, ranging from pocket books to pocket watches. Do they add or take away from your image as a professional? Again, young people seem to represent the extremes, but we adults have our foibles too. Once, I was shaking hands with the state president of a youth organization and my hand immediately grabbed what felt like a mother lode of rings. After releasing her hand, I noticed she had 5 rings on that one hand. On her arm she wore 3 or 4 gold bracelets, and each ear was pierced at least 4 times. I quickly inferred (whether correctly or incorrectly) that this young lady might be just a bit too caught up in external appearances. I realize I am walking on thin ice, but please remember my focus. Our goal is for the members of any organization to concentrate on the matters at hand, not marvel at the exorbitant way someone chooses to pierce their ear or body or decorate their digits (i.e. fingers). Young men have similar vices, like wearing their girlfriend's ring on a necklace. That is fine when in your home community or when not representing your organization, but to wear it outside your official dress so it is the first thing someone sees seems shallow at best. It says to me that the most important thing you want me to know about you as an officer is that you are in love with somebody, and your girlfriend wants you to use that ring as some sort of warning device to other women. Wear it, but put it inside your shirt. (After reading that, girls all over America will hate me I am sure!)

Your Odors

There, I said it. This may be a touchy subject for many, but since it hits home so often to me I must share it. I have a horrendous problem with bad breath. No matter how often I brush my teeth, the problem soon returns. Yes, I know it is coming from deep within my stomach, and there are many remedies, but none have seemed to work for me. What I have resolved myself to do is keep a case of sugar-free breath mints at home and grab a roll anytime I walk out the door on my way to be with people. Being a parent, they also work well as an incentive to a 2 1/2 year old to behave, but that is another book. Consciously I pop one in my mouth every one to 2 hours and it seems to work.

I bring this up because the most offensive thing in the world for me is to talk with someone whose breath says, "Here's what this person had for lunch." At meetings I normally sit in the audience until time to speak and usually sit next to some other dignitaries or key people up front in chairs that are way too close together. In many instances, I could not tell you a thing they said to me because the whole time I was trying to inhale at just the right time to avoid the smell. Sounds gross, but you have been in my situation before I'm sure. Part of my problem may result from hearing loss in my left ear, but with many individuals even being three feet away warns of impending danger.

When I speak to middle or high school groups, one of the biggest reactions I get to something I say comes when I ask the question, "Students, how many of you know a teacher here who has bad breath?" There is no hesitation. Hands shoot up like someone has asked for a volunteer to stay home from school for a week! While I have their attention I talk with them about the effects of "stinkin thinkin" and having a negative attitude. Teachers love to corner me after the program and rib me by saying, "You didn't ask *us* about the little darlings....we have 20 or 30 to contend with every day." I imagine I would get a similar response if I asked about fellow workers or officers in your organization.

Pack the breath mints or get a miniature bottle of mouthwash (not the ones that smell like alcohol; my wife said I smelled like I had been drinking before coming to the program). Do something to make it more pleasing for others to talk with you. If the problem is with the other person, take out your breath mints and discreetly (but noticeably) put one in your mouth. If the other person does not ask for one, offer them one. "They may be offended," you say. If your pants zipper were down or your blouse unbuttoned to your navel, would you be offended if someone told you? "Of course not, I'd want them to tell me because I don't want to look like an idiot." In my opinion, trying to carry on a conversation when your breath would drive Dracula away is no different.

Your Words

Abraham Lincoln once said, "It is better to be quiet and thought a fool than to open one's mouth and prove it." Wise words from our former president. Once beyond the rigors of our clothing and immediate appearance, our words speak volumes about who we are and greatly enhance or diminish our image. While presenting a workshop, I became quite disappointed with one of the participants. He was seemingly anti-everything and did not want to work together with the other participants. Since the workshop was on effective team building, his negative words created tension in the room. After attempting to talk with him during a break and having no success, I chose to speak with the executive director of the organization. His comment was, "Yes, that's our illustrious president." "Excuse me?" I said. "Yes, that's John. He carries that same attitude into our meetings, and it really detracts from any progress." No doubt. When the recognized leaders of an organization have a verbal viciousness about them, what does that supposedly say about the others? If these people are representative of the best ideals of the association, would we want to be a part of it?

One way to project a professional image with your words is to be positive about your role in the organization. Even if it is the most difficult task you have ever undertaken, do not share your horror story at every opportunity. Remember, you want others to *want* to be in your position in the future. Find an appropriate time to talk with the other leaders of the organization about your concerns in private. Airing your grievances to a group of people who do not know your organization (or the whole story so they will be more sympathetic) only serves to lessen the potential of that organization to attract quality people. Bashing the organization, its policies, or members will additionally lead others to question what you say about them when they are absent.

Secondly, refrain from "tooting your own horn." Success stories are needed in our world today (see chapter on adversity), but when you serve as a leader of a group or association, highlighting what you have done within the organization may be out of bounds. It sends signals to the group that their welfare is not important, that you are simply involved for what you can personally achieve. Please don't confuse this with communicating to others what the organization can do for them by your example. If you know much about me, you probably know that I served as a National FFA Officer, a position that was a major touchstone in my life. When talking with me, people will ask about it, and I am quick to say, "Yes, this organization gave me an opportunity to accomplish things I never thought possible." Help them see that it was the *group* that made it possible. Your talents and abilities played a role, but the organization was the critical element in the process. You want people to be an effective part of your *organization*, not your fan club. Highlight the accomplishments of the organization, its programs, and its members when possible. People already know you are an achiever by your position within the organization.

Refrain from inappropriate slang, profanity, or poor grammar. Sure, I use some Southern slang when appropriate in my programs but not until I believe the audience has a keen idea of who I am. Even then, it sometimes comes back to haunt me. In the Business Section of *The Charlotte Observer* a reporter had quoted some of my "country sayings" during a program to volunteers. Unfortunately, she included so many of them that someone reading the article might have gotten the idea that I was one more country bumpkin. Our use and abuse of the English language is crucial to creating a positive or negative image. I have an accent (I tell my Northern and Western audiences that they're the ones with an accent, not me) and have consciously worked to reduce my worst abuses. A comedian might exaggerate his/her accent for maximum effect, but those attempting to portray a professional image know the importance of cleaning up their words. Profanity (the wrong four letter words) has no place in anyone's vocabulary, in my opinion. After becoming a parent that became even more real to me. A neighbor was commenting on the goose droppings around our community pond. He said, "Look at all this goose _ _ _ _!" His three-year-old granddaughter immediately exclaimed, "Mommy, look at all this goose _ _ _ _!" Aside from giving children words they do not need to use, profanity reflects a limited vocabulary. Not that you have to choose five-dollar words to express emotion, but find something else to use. Even phrases like "anal retentive" are offensive to many people (including me) because they show an underlying, almost hidden, train of thought that can undermine one's respect for another. My thought is, "If they will use that language around total strangers, how much worse would it be around people they know?"

Finally, removing offensive jokes and comments from your verbal repertoire is important. As Patrick Grady says, "People just sit around waiting to be offended by something someone says." No matter how harmless the joke may seem, if there is an inkling that the joke may reflect negatively on who they are professionally or personally, watch out. "They need to get over it," you say. They indeed may need to be a little more secure about who they are, but your role as a leader is not to tear them down but rather to build them up. It is very difficult to gain the respect and trust necessary for organizational and relational growth if the other person (or group members) is suspicious of what you might say about them when they are absent from your presence. As that great philosopher, Thumper the Rabbit, said in *Bambi*, "If you can't say something nice, don't say nothing at all."

Your Actions

As a college student preparing to graduate in May, I sent out letters to perspective school systems inquiring about positions available as an agricultural teacher. One director of vocational education sent me a glowing letter challenging me to consider the opportunities of teaching in his county. I went for an interview and was amazed at his professionalism, vision, and ability to motivate others. Although I did not accept a job in his county, he always said he would call me if something developed more in line with what I was pursuing. It eventually did, and I began teaching in what I knew was going to be a wonderful location. The position turned out to be less than I had envisioned but was still a good place to teach. What bothered me more than anything, however, was the change in demeanor of the individual who had been so adamant about involving me in his vision. In a difficult time of adjustment, I rarely heard from him and would have greatly appreciated a word of encouragement. A visit, a call, or some other hint of that great enthusiasm he had shown before I became an employee could have seriously evened out the rough spots. All his words, whether written or spoken, were empty then as his true colors had been revealed by his actions.

We see it too much in our society. Whether we will admit it or not, we all want people to serve as our role models. Whether actors/ actresses, sports or political figures, or even the person down the street, we yearn for those individuals who espouse virtue and compassion and fight for the common good. Unfortunately, many of them may inspire us with grandiose words or perfect professionalism, only to burst our belief bubble with actions that contradict their seemingly positive image.

Sure, we all have trouble living up to our own words (practice what you preach), and people do have problems or circumstances that may force them to respond in a strange manner. What I am focusing on here is the deliberate attempt by others to appear to have one set of standards and motives, only to reveal a completely different set later by their actions.

As a speaker who travels frequently, I talk with many people. Some of them just seem to have a certain air about them, and we talk for long periods of time. They are very complimentary of my program. They talk about how they will achieve their goals and dreams and how they would like to stay in touch in the future. Handing them a business card, I count it a pleasure to have met them.

Several days later my phone will ring with this cheery person who will remind me of where we met, and once again my thoughts are positive. The next line goes something like this: "When you and I talked you said that you were always interested in new opportunities. Well my friends and I have started…" Yes, the network marketing people have struck again. When I politely try to tell them I am not interested, they talk of getting together for a few minutes just to look at the program. Not wanting to hurt their feelings (something I strongly espouse), I have normally gone and talked with them or visited their information meeting. As of yet, I have not seen anything in which I am interested. Strangely enough, once I reveal my intent to the individual, I never hear from them again. What happened to that nice cheery person who wanted so sincerely to keep in touch? Yes, they went on to manipulate someone else.

From being approached at an office supply store (the guy saw a copier as a way to start a conversation) to eating at a restaurant (the couple asked Alex's name to get their foot in the door) to someone asking me about the logo on my T-shirt, I do believe I have seen it all with these people. The results are always the same. If they cannot get what they want, they leave. What really infuriates me is the way they will use any angle possible to bait you. After I talked with one guy for several minutes, he inquired about my church and my involvement. He even said he might like to attend there one Sunday. I sent him information about the church and shared some of my personal beliefs, but I have not seen him yet.

Sadly enough, many of their products are sound ones. The method of delivery, however, leaves me with an image that will not soon go away. In all our endeavors, it seems essential to me to match our words with our actions. In this day of desire for the "scoop" on everyone from local politicians to fellow office workers to the President, no one is immune. How? Here is a thought.

Under Promise and Over Deliver. In his book *The Corporate Coach*, Johnny Miller gives an excellent explanation of this concept as it relates to the business world. In short, it means doing more than you said you would do. The tendency for many of us is to overcommit ourselves (over promise) and fail to follow through (under deliver) on our promise, resulting in a loss of respect by those to whom we made the commitment. As a father of a young daughter, I have experienced many instances of overcommitment. Alex loves to be read to, and Lisa and I try to fulfill her desire since it is such an important activity. She will ask about another book at bedtime, and we sometimes decline since it is a stay-awake tactic. Before retiring for the evening, however, I promise to read to her tomorrow morning. Things get hectic the next morning and at 10:00 AM (or later) I find myself saying, "In a minute," and actually getting to her 30 minutes later. She is normally patient and is waiting at the chair when Daddy gets done with his other stuff. As Alex gets older, though, she may not be as patient. Eventually, she may find something else to do since Daddy never seems to do what he says when he says it. With the concept of under promise and over deliver, I do not promise to read to her in the morning. When she gets up tomorrow, however, I will make arrangements in my work at home (get up a few minutes earlier) and be waiting with a book when she wakes up. The smile on her face is worth it all.

It makes us feel good to share our dreams, goals, and intentions with others. In the emotion of the moment, we share how important one person or a group of people are to our very existence. Our image is tarnished, though, when our actions continually do not line up with those verbal exhortations to others. As one observer says. "If you are on a diet, do not tell anyone...let them see the results." Under promise and over deliver.

Summing it Up

The image we convey is not something to be taken lightly. In the name of individuality or stereotyping we argue against such seemingly trivial things as our words and clothing. We have an excuse for not achieving any particular goal or for not meeting the commitments of a relationship. "It's okay," we say, "everybody does it." Yes, they may have started out in a similar predicament, but they have chosen to improve the perceptions others have of them in order to be successful in life, personally and professionally.

One of my values is to make a positive impact on the lives of others. Ultimately, I find that it is others who make a more positive impact on my life with their stories of hope, overcoming adversity and belief in others. If I refuse or fail to conduct myself in such a way that opens the door to a relationship (a positive impression), how will I ever get the opportunity to be a part of their life? Just like in dating to find that perfect mate, it is crucial that we constantly be putting our best foot forward to give a positive appearance. We should carefully consider our words to insure no misunderstandings or misconceptions. Having mastered these two areas, we continually strive to live up to our words through our actions. If not, the former two will be overshadowed by the latter, and we will have become like everyone else. I close with a quotation from Guy Doud, a former National Teacher of the Year:

> *"The eye is a more willing pupil than ever was the ear,*
> *Words are often confusing, but example is always clear."*

J

Jabber (Listening)

When I was growing up in Denton, I knew a wonderful old man named Jabber. He was always at the baseball games and many practices, giving advice and cheering on the young baseball players who were often less than spectacular (present party definitely included). This chapter has a strange connection to Jabber. Other than having the same name as this section, I remember him as someone who enjoyed helping us learn the game and was supportive of athletics in general. Jabber was an active participant in athletics instead of a passive supporter. This chapter is about being an active participant in listening.

In a world that boasts more communications capabilities than anytime in our history, listening has become a failed art, and we do a whole lot of jabbering instead. We hear the noise of talking but do little to actually process that information and use it in the betterment of professional and personal relationships. Instead of actively participating in the communications process, we hear all the noise, shout a few phrases at the appropriate (or inappropriate) time, and then fold up our mental yard chairs and go home to our own little world.

Why don't we listen? There are literally thousands of reasons, the kind of reasons that remind me of glass lenses. Ever picked up the wrong set of glasses? Once your headache goes away (the one caused by stumbling over an object you never saw), you realize that something is amiss. On a recent road trip I borrowed (without asking) a pair of my friend's sunglasses from the glove compartment. They were wonderfully clear and comfortable, and I planned to get a similar pair. When I inquired about the place of purchase, he replied, "The optometrist's office... they're prescription glasses with tinted lenses." Yep, time to get the contacts changed. Here are a few other lenses that may distort our listening capabilities:

· *Conflict lens:* Almost every word is evaluated on the idea that this person is out to wreak more havoc on our relationship and/or to me.
· *Insecurity lens:* Will something said make me less sure or secure in our relationship?
· *Suspicion lens:* I do not trust you. Why should I believe you?
· *Hurt lens:* If I have been hurt by someone in the past, I may listen for cues so that they will not hurt me again.
· *Ego lens:* Yes, there are those people who listen for the slightest words that may suggest that they are less than immortal.

You could probably make a list of your own. The key to all these is that at the point when I say something that meets the criteria (hurt, ego deduction, etc.), the other person begins preparing for verbal warfare. They sharpen their arrows of anxiety or anger while I am attempting to share why they should lay down their arms and yes, I have been on both sides of the fence, haven't you? (Nodding up and down indicates yes, turning your head left to right indicates no.)

I don't wish to turn this chapter a psychological quagmire of theories and processes, but what follows are some simple thoughts on getting others to actively listen to you and also to become a better listener yourself.

Getting the other person to listen

1) Build trust in the relationship. An ounce of prevention is worth a pound of cure. If the other person has a degree of trust in you and the relationship, you have set the foundation for productive discussions. A trusting person, mentally and emotionally comfortable, will typically listen much better. Look at the successful marriages around you. The level of trust in the other partner is so great that almost any controversial topic can be discussed because each spouse knows the deepest foundations of the other. Granted, such a relationship takes years to build, but even when dealing with our fellow employees and associates, a foundation of respect based on trust can go a long way in getting the other person to listen.

  2) Make sure the other person is comfortable and available to listen. Phrases like "Are you sitting down?" and "I need to talk with you" do not make me feel comfortable. Granted, some thick-headed individuals may need such an emotional slap in the face to jumpstart their participation in the discussion. If possible, though, find a moment when they are mentally and physically available. Approaching someone who is working at their desk but not with a client may seem like an opportune time. They may even respond "Yes" to a request for a minute of your time. Their mind, however, may be a million miles away. Getting to know the other person and their work habits may be helpful. Lisa does not ask me anything but the most vital questions while I am working on a speech. I am not on the phone or engaged in an active physical process, but her inquiries tear away at my mental concentration. Likewise, I do not make great verbal requests of Lisa when she is decorating a cake. It would seem to be something she could do without thinking, but again, pulling her focus from that task to another before she is ready may generate a negative response to a question.

  3) If a time must be set up to talk, be honest about the content. As the tired, old joke goes, "Know how to keep an idiot in suspense?... I'll tell you tomorrow." When we announce a need to talk, the other person's walls of defense may be triggered. Additionally, you may open a door of great expectations. Failing to remove the barriers or adjust the expectations may have dire consequences. At a conference not long ago a very influential man told me in passing that he needed to talk with me. His position included choosing several speakers for large meetings, and my heart leaped with anticipation as I expected him to select me for one or inquire about more information. Upon meeting at our appointed time, he revealed the opportunity... another network marketing product. I don't believe I heard a word once my hopes had been dashed. Granted, we do not need to share all our intentions, but to simply tell someone you need to talk with them at a scheduled time without revealing an inkling of the topic says to the other person, "What you might think about this situation is irrelevant. It is my viewpoint that is most important."

4) Use more phrases that include "I feel" and "for us" or "for the company" and less that include you, me, or "for your own good." Especially in conflict situations (see resolving conflict chapter), people are extremely sensitive about what you view as their shortcomings or failures. Focusing on how you feel or how it makes you feel (not pretending to have all the answers) keeps the doors of dialogue open rather than causing a resounding slam when you tell them what they are doing wrong. Looking at how actions (yours or theirs) affects the larger picture (marriage, company progress, etc.) also helps put things in perspective.

5) Follow up. After the conversation is over, make a mental note to talk with the person again within a short period of time to tie up loose ends and to discuss any questions or concerns that have arisen from your conversation. It may be as simple as seeing them in a hallway, making a friendly phone call, or sending a short note. Letting them know you are interested in them (and ultimately their thoughts) will create a more effective listener in future conversations.

Being an active listener

A little boy was enthusiastically learning how to ride his bike while his mother read her novel nearby. He shouted, "Mommy, look at what I am doing!" His mother, without raising an eyebrow, said, "Yes, I see you." The little boy, realizing something was amiss, said, "Mommy, how can you see me if your eyes aren't looking this way?" In defense of the mother, she had probably repeated this scenario hundreds of times and knew what the little boy wanted her to see...or at least assumed she did.

Listening is much the same process. We believe we know enough about the other person to understand their thoughts, so we anticipate their words without really paying attention. Beyond making good eye contact ("watch me Mommy"), there are other things that can increase our level of listening with another person:

1) Close your mouth. It is tempting, especially in emotionally charged conversations, to want to help the other person or to show them you know what they are going to say by finishing their sentence or commenting on every phrase. For me, the problem is that it breaks my train of thought (some would say it is still boarding at the station anyway). My belief is that if both of us can just get all our thoughts out, there is less danger of our getting caught up in one point or stopping the other person because something was said that one of us did not like. The common crowbar used to break into someone's strain of thought is the word "and." You are pouring your thoughts out to someone, and as you prepare to tell them the reasons behind your excitement (frustration, disappointment, etc.), they break in with "And you got the part in the school play!" It's like revealing the punch line to a favorite joke, leaving the other person feeling frustrated because they were the ones telling the joke.

It reminds me of the wife having car problems. The wife walked into the house and announced to the husband, "There's a problem with the car." The husband, having heard about squeaky doors and little rattles a hundred times, said, "Okay, what's the problem today?" She replied, "There's water in the carburetor." This got the husband's attention because now she was talking about his domain...the engine. He looked back at her and said, "What do you mean, there's water in the carburetor? You wouldn't know a carburetor from a C clamp!" The wife, feeling challenged, shot back, "Honey, I know what I'm talking about. There's water in the carburetor!" "Oh please," he whined, "I'll prove to you that there is no water in the carburetor. Give me the keys. Where's the car?" Her reply, "In our neighbor's swimming pool." When we interrupt people in mid-thought or attempt to get ahead of their words by finishing them, we may find ourselves feeling just a little awkward if things do not add up the way we assume they will.

2) Recognize gender differences. We will explore the differences between men and women later, but sufficient for now is the difference between the thought processes of males and females. Men seem to work best focusing on one issue at a time, while women can look at multiple issues at once and bounce around from one to another.

Depending on the situation, it may be important for one gender or another to come out of their normal mode of operation if the conversation is to go to a deeper level.

3) *Repeat their points in your mind.* I know this sounds psychological, but the main reason it works for me is because it prevents other things from distracting me. Studies have shown that we comprehend much faster than most people can talk or read. Think about it. While reading this book you have most likely been thinking of eight or ten different issues in your life. At the moment someone talks it may seem like gibberish, but our wonderful minds are storing that information and processing it in our subconscious. In the early 1980's a commercial for a shipping company used a man who talked so fast that it made my head spin. Ironically, I found myself understanding most of his words because I had to focus on what he was saying. Since most of us do not talk quite that fast, we need something to occupy the rest of our brain while part of it is processing our friend's comments. Repeating their words or key points in our mind while they are talking helps prevent being distracted by hunger or other work to be done.

4) *Focus your other energies.* Even after reining in your runaway mind, there are a couple other areas to consider. First, consider jotting down the key points shared by the other person. No, don't sit in a chair, legs crossed, and write down everything, but make some short jog phrases. Today many of our conversations originate on the phone. Writing notes to yourself about the discussion (not completing other work) can help keep you on target. It can also help with follow-up later.

Use of the wrong phone can also be a problem. Cordless phones are wonderful for their mobility but terrible for the quality of conversations. I don't mean reception either, but rather the tendency to try to do too many things at once. While talking, you can work outside, iron clothes, wash your car, prepare a meal or, yes, even visit the restroom. All this activity can detract from your ability to listen to the words on the other end. Your mind is now racing from one arena to another (did I put one cup or two cups of bleach in those clothes), and listening does not happen as effectively as it could if you were sitting down somewhere focusing on the conversation.

When I was growing up, my family did not have a phone until I was in the eighth grade. My cousins had a phone in their house, and I always thought it was the neatest thing to hear it ring, wondering who might be on the other end. Their phone sat on a little table in the hallway, away from everything. The only reason you would sit there was to talk on the phone. In the winter there was not much heat in the hallway, so you made the conversations brief and to the point.

Maybe putting a phone in the linen closet will not solve all our listening problems, but I do believe it will help us really concentrate on what someone is saying, as opposed to making their words part of the five other things we have going on at one moment. The same advice goes with cell phones, too. Trying to solve the world's problems while driving can create other ones. Nothing is more frustrating to me than hearing the momentary breakup that comes when someone is driving under a power line or similar interference when that someone is imparting critical information. Emergencies are one thing...calling to chat is another. Save it for a time when you can talk without swerving around that guy driving twenty miles an hour.

5) Stop sharpening your axe. We have all heard the phrase, "I have an axe to grind with you." It means I have a concern with you, and we need to talk about it. The problem is that we try to sharpen our words mentally while the other person is attempting to reconcile their differences with us. We can miss a key word of forgiveness or positive word because we are getting ready to do battle over something said 5 minutes or five years ago. When possible, hear them out. Even if they have wronged you in the past, give them an opportunity to explain themselves. Yes, if it is a pattern of behavior that has persisted for a long time, you may need to terminate the conversation before someone gets hurt.

6) Use phrases like "Help me understand." An extension agent I once met told me of an experience when she was a new agent in the area. She was deeply hurt by the actions of the group. Rather than get angry, she asked them to help her understand why they did it. She said the request disarmed them and allowed solutions to be secured for the future. In our conversations with others, it tempting to repeatedly use phrases like, "I know how you feel" or "I have been there." When someone says that to me, I often get the feeling that they simply want to lecture me or share their own story. Granted, that may be helpful in some cases, but frequently what I need is someone to ask *me* questions to help *me* clarify my thoughts. Some of the most engaging conversations I have ever had with people were ones where they asked for clarification on a comment in one of my presentations or in a discussion. It showed me that they were really listening and wanted to dig deeper into the issue. Even in periods of conflict, asking key phrases that take the conversation to a deeper level can do much to make the other person feel listened to and make them more comfortable sharing their true thoughts.

7) *Follow up. It appears on both sides of the coin.* When travelling in Tennessee several years ago, I met a man who worked as a teacher. As we talked, I asked him about future plans, and he told me of his dream to be the state advisor of a youth organization in 3-5 years. Later, I did see his name on a mailing that was leaving our office, so I wrote a note on the letter, congratulating him on his accomplishment. A call came a few days later and a voice said, "I cannot believe you remembered!" People appreciate knowing that we think about them and remember things shared in a conversation. It may be a call a week later, a note, or even a reminder about what was discussed when you see them later. It shows you really were listening and that the person has value to you.

Summing It Up

You may have noticed that there seems to be more we can do to be a better listener than there is to improve the listening skills of the other person. Surprised? I didn't think so. As much as we would like to, we cannot control and dictate the actions of another person. We can for awhile, but then they quit working for us, divorce us, or simply resent us forever (comforting thoughts, huh?). What we can do is attempt to be a better listener and provide the example (see image, last chapter) for them to follow. Remember, "Life is not a spectator sport." Sometimes you have to get in there and show them how to hit the ball.

K

Kites (Adversity)

"Remember, kites fly against the wind"

Overcoming adversity is a common theme in many talk shows, presentations and self-help books (like this one). Highlighting people's struggles to become more than they have been in the past is in vogue. Some people, however, have been mountain climbing over mole hills. They have embellished their fight to succeed in order to garner a greater favor. Amazingly enough, it is those individuals who rarely make the headlines who teach us the most about overcoming adversity. At least that is true in my life.

As I look back on my life thus far, I find little in the way of great adversity. I grew up in a proud little rural town where I walked to school (it was up a hill, but the hill was only three hundred feet long). The school was K-12, so I went to the same place every day with the same great friends, friends who taught, and continue to teach me much about life. I had model parents who saw to it that I had everything I needed and almost everything I wanted (did I mention that I was an only child?). Even on a modest income, they made everything work out and never came up short when it came to me. They both worked, but Daddy (the name for a real father in the South) or Mama kept me with them after school so I was not alone in the afternoons to get into trouble. Because of the upbringing by my parents and the positive influence of family and friends, I developed a strong desire to make the most of my life and was motivated to earn a college education, achieve many honors, and arrive at my current position in life. Okay, so maybe I'm bragging just a little, but I am simply a credit to all the people in my life who saw the need to make me who I am. I always strive to be a positive reflection of their efforts.

Oh sure, I could tell you about an automobile accident when I was two and a half (I went through the windshield, but only stitches and bruises resulted). Yes, and then there is the time I ran away from home (I was about 4 and got about 50 yards from the house). My bout with obesity comes to mind (I finally lost about 30 pounds in high school, and it did make a difference), or we could talk about my inferiority complex (once while singing in the church choir as a junior high student, the football team came to the service. I just knew they would call me a sissy.). Seriously, though, I have had several things that I consider "adverse" conditions in my life. We all do, and this chapter is about that type of adversity. It has also been my privilege to be associated with many people who have overcome life-threatening adversities, and some you will read about here. Their stories, combined with ours, form a type of think tank (a trendy term) from which we can glean strategies on getting our own kites to fly.

As I was thinking about adversity, I went to the dictionary for a clearer definition. One definition I found referred to "adverse" as "opposing or contrary." Looking above the word in the dictionary, I saw the word adversary, which means "opponent." With adversity, it made sense to me that overcoming it means overcoming one or more opponents, opponents to getting where you want to be in life (not just overcoming possible death or dire situations). The possibilities are numerous:

- Physical/Mental Handicaps - These are most readily recognized in our society and, amazingly enough, are the ones that people most often seem to overcome.

- Financial Constraints - Seed money for a new business, funds for college, or just making ends meet may be holding us back.

- People who are threatened by your potential success - Yes, fellow employees may not always cheer for your desire to grow and classmates in high school or college do not necessarily have kind words to say about your willingness to commit yourself to higher standards. They are not interested in rising above the status quo.

- Your insecurity - Scared of where a new direction may lead? Perhaps seizing the opportunity will require you to step out of your comfort zone.

- Insecurity of other people - Significant others, parents, or friends may fear the effect your change will have on your relationship with them, especially if the relationship is not stable.

- Perfectionism - Feeling overwhelmed because you are anxious about how well you can actually perform a new task.

- Time - Putting things off until later often means never tackling them at all.

- Present circumstances - Unfavorable anything: Parents, relationships, hometown opportunities, weight, etc.

Again, you can add any number of things to the list, but you get the picture.

Having helped (hopefully) you see that adversity is not just hanging off a cliff on a limb that is quickly breaking, let's explore some possible avenues to getting to our destinations.

1) Have the goal in mind. A popular observation about risk is, "A ship in harbor is safe, but that is not what ships are made for." If we have no goals, then we should have no adversity. Indeed, the fear of failure may play a major role since we are afraid that if we have higher expectations we may fail to reach them. Having a goal in mind may seem a trivial place to start, but we have all met people so overwhelmed by their circumstances and other opponents that they choose simply to sit and watch the world go by. Perhaps we have even been there ourselves.

2) Identify your true opponent(s). In the TV show *Walker, Texas Ranger*, Chuck Norris plays the main character. He wins many of his battles using the martial arts (against some real weak competition). It is interesting to watch as he positions himself near the center of a room or near the middle of the group of villains. As they approach him, he takes out the guy closest to him first, then works on the others as the situation deems necessary. He does not, however, run to the guy furthermost away and start throwing leg kicks at him. If he did, the others would surely "clean his clock" because he failed to take care of them first.

When overcoming adversity, identify the opponent most immediately facing you. Looking too far down the road may cause you to get ambushed now by something you missed. A member of our church community had a little boy nearly the same age as Alex. Soon after he was born, the mother indicated the desire to stay home with her son beyond the normal six weeks. When we asked about why she could not, her reply was, "We have too many bills." Being a close friend, we began to inquire further, attempting to help her find possible solutions. As we dug deeper, we discovered her true opponent... her relationship with her husband. Because of a lack of compassion in the relationship, he saw no need to change some of his excessive spending habits. Additionally, the couple lacked the communication skills that would have helped them really discuss her goals as it related to staying with her son. It is easy to put a seemingly immovable mountain in front of us to prevent us from seeing the root of our adverse situation. Recognizing the real problem would place climbing out of debt secondary. Improving the relationship with the husband would now be first in line. Similarly, getting a scholarship for college might at first appear difficult because of your choice of majors. Looking deeper, however, your first adversary might actually be your lack of commitment to improving your grades.

3) Determine your resources. Here is the stumbling block for the masses. After identifying the obstacles in our way, we say, "What can I do about them?" Merely relying on our own knowledge and abilities may limit the answers, leaving us depressed and ready to trash the goal. Beyond individual resources, look to enlisting other people in your adversity army. Because of pride and/or a fear of appearing weak, we refrain from seeking the wisdom of others. In the back of our minds, however, we hope they will come bursting through the door and save us from our misery. One of my favorite phrases to others is, " I will help you anyway I can, but I cannot read your mind." That comment is a two-edged sword. It implies that the other person needs to tell me what they need. It also indicates that I need to be close enough to them to hear what they are telling me (or not telling me).

Excluding other people in our search for success also creates another danger. If we fail in our quest, who will be there to pick us up? Who will sustain us in our time of greatest need? If we have stomped their fingers when climbing over them on the ladder of success, why should they reach out to catch us when we fall? Yes, those people with hearts as big as life will scrape us off the pavement, but what about others who might not only pick us up but also point us in the right direction when we have lost our way?

In one of my presentations to youth groups, I use a small trash can with four foam balls. After securing two volunteers, I station one behind the trash can, which is usually sitting in a chair. The other person stands in front, about three feet away from the trash can. Handing them the four balls, I tell them to perform the difficult task of "shooting" the foam basketballs into the trash can (the other person is a human backboard). They look strangely at me (a common response) but immediately shoot at least three out of four balls into the can. Cheering wildly for them, I talk about such a great achievement (strange look returns). Next, I have them change places. My new recruit is poised and ready when I say, "Okay, now back up just a little." They take one baby step back, only to be encouraged to step back more until I have them 10-12 feet away from the trash can. I tell them to expect the same results. You know what happens. At best, they get one basketball in the trash can. I then discuss the difference between taking the easy way out (setting small goals like passing your classes) and striving to reach a level of excellence (all A's and B's). The response is sometimes that at least the first person reached more of their goals. Yes, they do. But are they really meaningful? Do they really reflect what we want from life? Having said that, I set the stage again. This time my long-distance shooter takes their position away from the basket. My first basketball star now holds the trash can, still standing 10-12 feet away from the other person. The instructions to him go like this: "When he shoots the ball this time, move the trash can to a location where the ball will go into it." The shooter normally gets a minimum three out of four.

Involving other people in our efforts to overcome adversity is much like the long-distance shooter with the moving basket. When we involve other people's experiences, wisdom, and resources (the person moving the basket), it becomes much easier to reach a point in life that seemed difficult before. Most people do want to help... but cannot read your mind.

When we moved into our current home, one of our first tasks was to remove fallen limbs and a few trees from the property. Loading up my truck, I drove to the corner of the lot and dumped the limbs and logs. Upon attempting to drive out, I became mired up in Union County mud. After trying all the usual tricks (rocking, boards under the wheel, etc.), I saw it was no use. I hooked up our car to the truck and tried to pull it out, but no go. This truck was planted. "What am I going to do?" I thought. "The closest person I know is twenty minutes away." I thought about a tow truck, but as you can read in my money management chapter, I hate spending money to make up for my stupidity. Lisa and I decided to go in the house and have lunch (eating always puts things in perspective... and now you know why I need to lose twenty pounds). In a few moments the sound of four-wheeler came from our back door. There stood a husky guy who looked similar in age to me. Before I could say a word, he stuck his hand out and said, "My name is Sammy and you need my help." Being the typical male (see xy chapter), I wanted to tell him no, but he was right. I agreed to let him take the four-wheeler around back and hook up to the truck. He wanted to go get the tractor, but I insisted that he try the four wheeler first (I did not want to inconvenience him anymore than I had to). After several strong tugs, it became evident that the tractor would be necessary. In a few moments he was back with the tractor and dragged the truck from its mucky demise. We all have times when we are stuck in the proverbial ditch. To me, denying others the opportunity to help us get out is actually a sign of weakness. It says to me that you believe you will never be able to help me or anyone else in a similar manner in the future. Since that day when Sammy pulled me out of the mud, there have been many instances when he has helped me in other ways. Ironically, as we have gotten to know each other, I have assisted him with some adversity of his own from computer work to a demo video for his company's products to assisting with work on the farm. Enlisting Sammy's help in my adversity has led to a relationship where we each have a valuable resource to call on in times of need.

　　4) Plan your attack. With resources in hand, lay out a course of action. Be very specific, however, in what you plan to do. Saying, "I will try to do better" or "Yes, I want to ＿＿＿＿＿＿" fails to utilize your resources. If I want to lose twenty pounds, simply saying, "Yes, I will cut back on my intake of sweets" is not enough. I must take some specific steps to see that my plan is carried out. First, I might tell Lisa to refrain from buying my favorite cookies (if they have sugar in them, they are my favorite). I might also plan to stop eating anything after 8:00 PM at night. The more specific the plan, the better the opportunity to evaluate our progress and readjust when necessary.

　　Darrell was a few years younger than me. Growing up in southern Davidson County, Darrell was the kind of guy a teacher would love to clone and fill their classes with everyday. He was sometimes quiet but always enthusiastic. He had a winning smile and a positive attitude that was evident in everything he did. Darrell grew up poor, though, and had a large family whose members were not always as positive as he. While at a school function one day, I overheard Darrell say he wanted to be a lawyer. Mentally, I applauded his goal but shrugged it off thinking, "How will he ever go that far?" I knew he was a nice young man, but a lawyer? Beyond the money, how would he ever get into law school? What unfolded next is still a testament to the human spirit and a model for me. Darrell worked hard in high school, keeping up his grades, and got involved in extra-curricular activities that helped his social skills. Because of his commitment to his studies, Darrell got some financial assistance for college and chose to go to North Carolina State University. I inquired about him soon after his entering college and was told he was getting married. Married? "This will be the nail in the coffin," I thought. No one could juggle a full course load, part time work, and a marriage. Darrell did. After he graduated from N.C. State, I learned of his acceptance into the School of Law at the University of North Carolina. Darrell is now a practicing lawyer in my (our) hometown of Denton, N.C. Darrell was successful because he always had a plan of attack. Anytime I inquired about him, his friends would say, "You know Darrell, he has a plan for everything." Perhaps not everything can be so simply laid out, but organizing a plan is a good place to start.

One of my favorite subjects to teach in Agricultural Education was woodworking. The common plan was to teach the safe use of the shop equipment, how to read a measuring tape and how to complete a project. Before entering the shop each student had to choose a wood project displayed in class and sketch it out on paper, with a bill of materials listing all the parts and their dimensions. I allowed them to modify the dimensions to fit a specific need if necessary. They would be graded on how well their project matched up to the one sketched on paper. I was overall always pleased with their ability to follow the plan and to complete a project that showed good effort and was something they could be proud of for years to come.

As they finished their first project, I would allow them to start a second one. This time, however, they were to create one without a model, coming up with all dimensions and specifications. Again, they would be graded on how well their project matched up to the one created on paper. Let the games begin! One student, who originally planned to build a shelf for his room, wound up with a flat board in which he had inscribed his name with a router. Another student who had planned to make a cedar chest wound up with a cedar surfboard (don't ask). The list goes on and on. What made the difference? In the first project they had had a model and had specific steps that had been taught, tested, and demonstrated by me. In the second project, they had to go on their newly acquired skills and their ability to create a plan of their own. Lacking a concrete plan, the students were subject to change their direction frequently due to their moods, peer pressure or failed attempts at a woodworking technique.

Perhaps you are a self starter who can head off in any direction and accomplish what you set out to do. I, however, need a model. I need someone who has blazed a similar path or has some skills or abilities that I can emulate to accomplish my own project. Without that, I find myself constantly changing plans that show little congruency with the original concept.

5) Ask yourself, "What is the worst thing that can happen if pursue this plan of action?" Will a sincere attempt that fails really leave permanent scars on your life, or will it just bruise your ego? Lisa and I both are speedy drivers on the road. However, we are constantly careful about exceeding a safe speed that will endanger Alex or someone else in the vehicle. We have a more shallow reason, too. Getting a speeding ticket would send our insurance rates through the roof (and you know how I hate to spend money on my own stupidity). I have a friend, though, who thinks nothing of passing cars at a blistering speed at a moment's notice. He also has connections at the district attorney's office. Some people may be able to take chances or risks that seem like a foolish path for us. Because of some available resource, whether fair or not, however, their plan of action may not represent a valid one for us to follow.

6) Commit to your plan for a defined period of time. When wearing seat belts first became a law in North Carolina, the Department of Transportation issued a plan to help people remember to buckle up. You were to sit in your car (while parked in your yard) and fasten and unfasten your seat belt ten times. Psychologically, it was to burn it into your memory with each time you repeated the task. It worked for me. My neighbor saw me and asked if I was doing a new dance called the "Seat Belt Boogie." When we try to overcome those difficult situations in our lives, we must give ourselves an open window of time to get things moving and to properly evaluate our decisions. Failing to do so causes our memory to scream back at us later, "What if you had stuck with it?" or "You must be a failure since you could not stay with it longer than that."

As you may have read earlier, Lisa had a terrible first year of teaching. Because of many external negative circumstances, she was ready to pack it in and go somewhere else. We interviewed in several places, but something kept nagging at her to stay with it. She decided to stay for another year and sincerely attempted to make things better. When things continued to fall down around her, the decision to leave was much clearer. Having left after that first year would have caused

Lisa to later wonder about the potential for success if she had stayed for a second year. Having stayed for it, her conscience was much more at rest.

Our impatience gets the best of us. Many small businesses fail because the owners are frightened by the duration of negative revenue (i.e. length of time they lose money). If they thought it was so easy, they should have looked around. Was everybody doing it? People fail to stop smoking or kick other bad habits because they try it for a few hours, and it is uncomfortable. It seems ironic that many of us believe a behavior that has been engrained into our being for several years can be wiped out in just a few moments. Committing to doing something means sticking with it even when the emotional high of making the decision has ebbed. If we have aptly identified our resources (see number 2), then we have individuals or groups who can sustain us in those dark moments when we want to light up, eat a doughnut, or even throw away a marriage.

7) *Don't break out the autograph pen just yet.* So you have just triumphed over your worst fears or accomplished a most difficult endeavor. You call a press conference to discuss how you did it. You step up to the podium and see an audience full of… empty seats. Maybe the weather was just not conducive, or maybe people in general are pretty insensitive. Maybe as a father and teacher, I have been amazed at the way we reduce our level of enthusiasm toward another's accomplishments as we get older. Now that Alex is two and a half, Lisa and I find ourselves reinforcing her for everything from identifying the right color to properly using the potty and knowing her address. Our family and friends also praise her (she deserves it) for her accomplishments. During their first years in school, children are applauded for listening, correctly writing their letters, and knowing their multiplication tables. As high school students they will be rewarded for efforts in completing a ten page essay, achieving in sports, and choosing the right person to date. Later, they will excel in a job, build a family, and provide nurture and care to their own family. All the while, the number of people who will be cheering them on seems to diminish, while the accomplishments seem more extraordinary. It's just a fact of life that as we get older, the drive to excel goes from a predominately external one (praise

of others) to a more internal one (self-worth). Getting praise from others, however, feels good at any age, especially in our adult years when the obstacles have become much more complex and numerous.

Unfortunately, *60 Minutes* will probably not knock at your door wanting an interview on your tremendous accomplishment of losing thirty pounds, or kicking the smoking habit, or even being successful in a difficult career. The majority of the rewards will be intrinsic in nature, holding meaning only to you and a few other people. "Virtue is its own reward."

From a career success perspective, nothing had more meaning to me than the day Lisa came home from work for the last time. Even writing about it now I get all mushy inside. Though it seemed like a huge accomplishment to Lisa and me, few people even said congratulations. While it hurt at the moment (we all like to have our egos stroked), I quickly got over this lack of appreciation. The look in my wife's eyes each morning as she hurries about the house helping me and looking after Alex means more than any plaque or pat on the back from anyone. Whether a product of people's jealousy or indifference, always expect the party to celebrate your accomplishments to be a small gathering.

A Warning

Watch out for those who seek to constantly tell you of their accomplishments, large or small. The key word here is "constantly." As a speaker, I find myself being the sounding board for many who want to show off their greatness. The high point for me in many of my programs is conversing with individuals about their life stories, dreams, and plans for the future. Their stories are tremendous in many cases, and I count it a privilege to have met them. Some, however, must believe I am forgetful, that I will not inquire about who they are. Recently, while being transported from one part of a state to another by car, I listened (for over two hours) to a man highlight his accomplishments from high school to travel in a foreign country to his current job position. By the time we got to our destination, I was ready to scream. I tried to act like I was sleeping, but even that did not stop him. It seemed that at every opportunity he was expounding upon the greatness of his accomplishments. Even when I tried to change the subject, he always rolled back to himself. What? You say you know this person. Well, there's more than one in this world.

A mental red flag goes up in my mind when I'm in the presence of people who are more interested in highlighting their accomplishments than in genuine dialog (notice: The prefix dia means more than one). It says to me that they have some hidden, unfulfilled desire or achievement that they are afraid I might inquire about if we really talk. The goal is to keep my input to a minimum so the conversation can keep them in a favorable light. I'm not perfect by any standard, and do not expect others to be either.

I also feel a sense of compassion for these people since I believe they are insecure about some relational aspect of their lives. Job accomplishments may mask troubles in a marriage. Constantly talking about your children may hide the desire for a more enriching life for the mother (or father) who spends such an inordinate amount of time raising them. Life for such people is like an obstacle course, except they choose which obstacles they want to address and which ones they want to skip. The result? They will never win the prize of a full, well-rounded life. Like a bed with a spring jutting through the mattress, something will never feel quite right.

A Final Thought

Adversity comes in all shapes and sizes. For some it may be getting up in the morning, while for others it may be surviving as a missionary in a foreign country. No matter what the situation, enlisting the help of others, carefully planning our course of action and being our greatest fan (rejoicing privately and humbly in our accomplishments) can go a long way in overcoming any opponent.

L

Luck

"Luck Is When Preparation Meets Opportunity"

If you have been searching for a brief chapter to read when you are waiting in line or only have a few minutes to fill with a worthwhile activity (see time management chapter), this is it. I personally refrain from using the word "luck" at all costs. The reason? It implies no (or at least very little) responsibility on our part. Luck relies on external circumstances to form our happiness or unhappiness. It is my personal belief that we have a tremendous personal accountability in insuring our future success, which relies very little on external circumstances. In fact, blaming everything on good luck or bad luck seems to deny us the opportunity of appreciating our own talents and abilities, which can have a far greater impact on the success of our endeavors.

This is not to say that I would not accept a large check from a sweepstakes entry or a new car from a free drawing. The only thing I have ever won by luck in my life is a hunting bow. Even then my mother had bought several raffle (donation) tickets to bolster my chances. There's the word I was searching for, chance, a word that means "happening once." Opportunity, on the other hand, may knock a little more frequently, especially if we are prepared to open the door. Let's look at the definition of luck a little deeper.

When Preparation Meets Opportunity

Many people live their lives hoping that luck will swing in their favor and make their lives wonderful. It rarely happens. The success stories of musical stars who were once waitresses or construction workers seem to imply that luck is a viable resource. However, when we explore many of their stories later, we find that they had been honing their singing skills for years before becoming an "overnight sensation." Getting into the college of your choice may seem like a lucky happenstance, but reflect back on your struggle to make good grades. You were preparing to meet an opportunity. I have a friend who will be getting married soon. Talking with some friends, I heard one say, "He was really lucky to find her," like it just happened that they met. I reminded him of all of the future groom's years preparing for that one day by maintaining high moral standards and becoming a well-rounded person. A blind date, planned date, or even dating service could not have kept these two together this long without prior preparation in their own lives.

Teachers can tell you all kinds of stories of students who hope to use luck as their ticket to the stars. "I have an uncle who works in construction" or "My brother knows someone who can get me a job at the plant making $15 an hour." Those phrases are often interjected into a conversation where the teacher is attempting to get a student to take a subject more seriously. "I don't need to know how to do this stuff. I am going to be a _____." One of my wife's students was similar in thought. No matter how hard Lisa tried, it was like pulling eye teeth to get him to focus on learning a new skill. He was going to get a job through a friend who made good money at a local assembly plant. Near graduation another teacher told him of a local employer who was looking for a new person to learn the operation of new equipment. While the pay was not as good, the skills learned would be invaluable, and the young man would be in high demand in the area. "But, I already have a job lined up," he said. Less than one year later, he hated his perfect job and was frustrated to find that his marketable skills were limited, especially at a level of pay he wanted to earn. No preparation, no opportunity.

We adults do little better. We want the opportunity, and *then* we will prepare for it. We want a better job but want someone to give it to us (luck), and then we will do the work necessary to be successful. It's like preparing for a hurricane. I marvel at the news reports showing people preparing for a hurricane along the East Coast. Plywood over the windows, tying down anything that can be flung into the air, getting out of town as quickly as possible. And then we learn about a few locals who are going to weather the storm. They simply remain in their homes, laughing at the thought of any danger. More than once the story has turned tragic. As the hurricane approaches, they realize that this one is for real and attempt to be saved by radioing anyone who will listen and heed their cry. Unfortunately, their call will come too late for anyone to save them, and they perish in the storm. No preparation, no opportunity. In this case, no preparation (i.e. leaving or going to a storm shelter) meant no opportunity to continue living. Tragic as well to me is what happens to people who keep putting off doing things in their life, waiting for the opportune moment. When that moment does arrive, however, their situation dictates that they must pass it up because they have not made appropriate preparations.

The Triviality of Luck

Beyond preparation and opportunity, another fear strikes me when we attribute so much to chance. We hear others say, "I'm so lucky to have so and so as my spouse" or "He's lucky to be alive." One might as well rub my face with sixty grit sandpaper. My choice of words for those situations would be "blessed" or "fortunate." First of all, blessed recognizes a higher power and a degree of personal responsibility. If I have been blessed with something, then I must take care of it or them in any way I can. "Fortunate" would also be a better word to use than luck because it implies something very valuable (fortune). If I have been fortunate enough to land a good job, then I must work to deserve that fortune. Investing it wisely (i.e. being a good employee) and protecting it (improving my skills) are just a couple of ways to make sure that it does not quickly stray from my grasp.

Okay, I know some of you are screaming, "But, Jones, we can't control everything!" I wondered how long it would take you to bring that up. Yes, there are many things in our lives that we cannot control.

Being a victim of downsizing in a corporation is one example. Having a less than competent set of parents is another. A world of things can happen to us over which we have little control and that leave us hanging our heads in despair or disgust. In my opinion, we must simply prepare for our futures in every way we humanly can. From maintaining a level of moral purity to getting a good education (through an institution or the workplace) to constantly improving our relationships with family and friends, we can do much to take the guesswork out of life. As for the things we cannot foresee and that negatively affect our being, we have two options. One is to count it as adversity (see kite chapter) and start working to get back on track. Another thought (not secondary in importance, however) is to have faith in God. If you want more information about that, see the zeal chapter.

M

Money Management

This is a chapter I would not have expected to find in a book on getting the most out of life. It seems shallow to talk about something as concrete as money when the other chapters tackle such abstract concepts. However, I have come to realize that all the other parts of building a successful life can be in place (goals, abilities, relationships), but without the proper management of one's financial resources it's like a sled with no snow. Things just will not move in the direction we need them to go.

There was an older man who went to the doctor. His complaint? He had swallowed a twenty-dollar gold piece. When diagnosing the problem, the doctor asked, "How long ago did you swallow the money?" "Two years ago," the patient replied. "Two years ago!" exploded the doctor. "Why did you wait two years to see me?" The old man's reply, "Well, I didn't need the money until now." That pretty much sums up many people's ideas about money management. They will spend it as they wish, regardless of upcoming events or circumstances in their lives. When those situations occur, however, they panic about where they will find the funds to meet the current crisis. Often, in our lives, the money is not there, and we must respond to the situation in a way that is not in our best interest or in which our goals and dreams must be sacrificed.

On the road I meet people who have a desire to pursue a career similar to mine. I get excited if they have technical expertise in an area that will prove invaluable in developing their presentations and marketing themselves to various groups. When they talk about their area of interest, they have a certain sparkle in their eye and an ever-present grin on their faces that tells me they are passionate about it and will no doubt be successful. Getting beyond the actual presentations, we begin to talk about the business itself. The proverbial shoe drops when I tell them about depending on their spouse's income or personal savings for one or two years. As a result of earlier financial obligations and poor decisions, they cannot run such a risk. Seeing them one or two years later, I often inquire about where they are in their plans. The gleam in their eye gone now, they say it's just too far out of reach. To bottom line it (a good financial term), it scares me to think about anyone missing out on all life can be because of poor financial planning or decisions. Granted, just because we properly put away our pennies does not mean we have a free ticket to the world, but it does allow us more flexibility in making decisions about our career, family and opportunities that may come our way.

Yes, I feel your tug on my ear. "Jones, not all situations dealing with money can be controlled so easily." Once again, you may move to the front of the class. Natural disasters, downsizing, or a death or illness in the family are just a few things that can turn our financial coffers upside down. College loans that must be paid back quickly are another strain on our efforts to become more focused in our spending and saving. Special medical assistance for ourselves or for our children may be an ever-present need in our lives. Even a poor start in life due from poverty or parents who could provide little in the way of support can hamper our desire to get the most out of life. Going back to my philosophy on adversity, however, I believe that you first of all have faith in God and second use that strength to control the things you can. All the insurance policies in the world do not insure future financial well-being. Our world changes quickly today. Mutual funds amassed to levels in the billions can be wiped out in a single day.

People will also look to deprive you of your financial freedom. If you get into your car and drive down the block and rearend someone's car, you could potentially be out millions of dollars if the right circumstances are present. When I'm speaking, if I offend someone by using a joke or story that places that person in a negative light, I am open to litigation. Charges that could eventually cause me to lose my house and any amassed wealth.

In addition, easy obtainment of wealth causes its own problems. In June 1983, a previously private company called Eagle Computer went public. Its President, Dennis Barnhart, made nine million dollars in the initial public offering (IPO). He was so excited about his new-found wealth and success that he bought a new red Ferrari to celebrate. On the way home he was driving too fast, the car went through a guardrail, and Dennis Barnhart plummeted to his death in a ravine below. His company died along with him. Just because you can afford a Ferrari does not mean you know how to drive it.

On a higher level, we might say that sometimes success comes so quickly we are not prepared for it and make foolish mistakes that take our wealth almost as fast as we accumulate it. Tony Dorsett was an all pro running back for the Dallas Cowboys in the late 1970's. Being a Pittsburgh Steeler fan at the time, I had little to do with the Cowboys but admired the grace and agility of Tony Dorsett. The Steelers had Franco Harris, a huge bull of a man who could hit a car and move it ten feet. Dorsett, however, had a style about him all his own and was one of the highest paid players in his day. I had not heard about Dorsett in years until recently. At last report he was living in Texas, penniless and practically homeless. All his wealth gone, he is at the mercy of those around them. You say, "Goodness, if I had earned all that money, there's no way I would have thrown it away." Maybe you wouldn't, but the odds say most of those around you would.

Look at people fresh out of college. Having survived on macaroni and cheese or delivery pizza for many years, they finally enter the working world with a steady income. First comes a new vehicle and then amenities for their new living space. "Why bother to cook when I can go out and eat?" they ask. Soon, all that seemingly endless income each month has become just enough to get by. Saving can wait until later. A few years later, their standard of living has become so high that they are deeply drowning in debt, trying to figure out how to meet next month's bills. Their lack of long term money management has doomed them to failure.

Inheritance or quick money can also ruin us. A friend of mine lost her parents while she was still in college. They had provided well for her, however, and she was set for life if she simply invested the money in a secure, slow-growth fund or annuity. She met a guy she later married, and they settled down. Or so I thought. Removed from the pressures of working, they quit their jobs and quickly moved to an area with a high cost of living. They started a home-based business with little pre-planning or investigation into its success in the market place. New vehicles appeared, and life was good. Soon, however, they were forced to sell their property. A second child came along. Not having heard from them recently, I have no idea of the stage of their demise. Hopefully, they will, with the support of friends and family, be able to regroup before the money is gone. If not, my fear is that the marriage and the children are in grave danger. You probably know people in your community who have inherited wealth and went on to increase its value even more. It does happen, but even many of them will tell you it was not the bed of roses some might think. Some use the fast cash to pay off loans or credit cards, only to get into the same (or worse) financial obligations when the money is gone.

This chapter will focus on two specific areas of money management: Preventing financial turmoil and getting out of financial turmoil. You are now rummaging through my biography to determine my experience as a financial planner. I'll save you the trouble. Except for a few months experience with a certified financial planner (I had considered pursuing it as a part time job but saw quickly I could not split my efforts), I have little professional expertise to share with you. My thoughts have two primary sources. One is my own life, which has had a few financial bumps along the way, and the other source is the financial successes of those around me. Stories of people like Donald Trump or Ross Perot or Ted Turner offer great insights into becoming wealthy. However, many of their strategies may seem a bit beyond the understanding of the rest of us. By looking around you, you will no doubt see individuals like yourself who *are* achieving their financial goals. Look at their example. If they are your friends, ask them how they did (or are doing) it. Even then, you may not get answers that you can take to the bank (I just had to throw that in), but at least you have a wealth of ideas and strategies that you can modify and perhaps implement in your own life almost immediately. Of course, if they have a heavy traffic flow in and out of their driveway and the blinds are always pulled at night and they are constantly receiving shipments from South America, you may not want to inquire in great detail. The police might just show up while you are conversing in the living room and mistake you for a client. (i.e. Your neighbor was a drug dealer.)

Preventing Financial Turmoil
Under 16

Get a part-time job. Seem trivial? Guess again. Even if your financial source (parents/guardians) supplies your immediate needs, put yourself in the working world. Get an early sense of what it feels like to have responsibility. Commit yourself either to save the money or spend it on certain items in your life. Doing so lets you see how easily it can be exhausted and can help you gain a greater appreciation for spending it wisely.

When I was ten, I began mowing two yards. Nothing huge, just something to do for a couple hours a week. By the time I was 16, I had 5 or 6 yards along with numerous other odd jobs. I cleaned cars, worked on farms, and even helped in cemeteries. I was also a delivery boy for a furniture store. With the money I had earned at 15, I bought a truck for $350 dollars. No, it was not much, but it was a symbol of accomplishment for me that has remained with me to this day. Even though that was years ago, I still believe there is a market for young people to work in such arenas. The beauty of this type of work is that they have more flexibility in working hours and can still function as a high school student. It bothers me to see so many young people find their first job at a fast food restaurant or similar location. The hours are often unkind, including work on weekends. It's actually like a full-time job. The money seems good, so they make sacrifices in other areas to keep the job. Grades slip and participation in the joys of high school life (sports, socializing, organizations) take a back seat to make room for being a working man or woman. Granted, if you must work to support your family, then it will be justified. Working, however, simply to gain, gain, gain, only sets you up for a distorted view of the purpose of work later in life.

Say you're lazy? Technology has helped there, too. Now yards are groomed with self-propelled push mowers or cushy riding mowers. Most windows in newer homes today have no storm windows, so cleaning them is much easier. After school care is another easy option. Yes, chasing that seven-year-old around the house may not seem easy, but look at all the exercise you're are getting. Employers, whether they be a single parent or a local used car lot operator, seem to be looking for people like you who want part time work. They only need a few hours here and there, and are often flexible if you do a good job. The key is getting out there and asking. Do one job and do it well, and you will turn away work. One young lady in my church started babysitting for one family a few years ago when in high school. I called her a few months later because the mother raved about what a great job she did. I was shocked and somewhat disappointed that two or three families had her on permanent hold. Even now when she is home from college on some weekends, she is in great demand as a babysitter.

Save some money. I am a fiscally conservative kind of guy. My wife jokes that when I was slapped on the bottom to begin crying as a newborn, I looked at the doctor and said, "Do you charge extra for that?" For me, saving money even at an early age was not difficult. My parents did a great job teaching it to me, and somehow it stuck. If you, are the kind of person who must spend a dollar if you have it, however, find a way to delay that instant gratification. Many banks still offer a type of "Christmas Club." You simply put a defined amount in each week, and it accumulates until December of that year. You then receive a check for all the money you have deposited into their account. No, it does not draw interest, but if you are currently spending your cash anyway, what concern is interest to you? Just having money later is a step in the right direction. Parents or other family members can also be your banker in those cases.

If college is in your future, perhaps a savings account would be in order to draw some interest. Even if the interest is minimal, building up those funds now gives you a source of early financial freedom when you get to college. No, it does not pay for tuition costs or books, but it might provide for the once-a-week delivery pizza or a trip to the mall from time to time.

Examine your career choice. Being older now, I have come into contact with countless students I went to college with or even taught during my early years as an educator. When they tell me what they are doing now, my mind quickly retrieves their previous plan for success to check for congruency. If incongruencies do exist, it is usually because the job was not all it was cracked up to be. Almost as often, however, is the complaint that their original career choice did not meet their financial needs. To see if your career choice will measure up, find an older friend who seems to be taking their life in the direction you want to go. They should have a home similar to one you hope to have and similar family size and amenities (cars, hobbies, etc.). Have them go over their weekly, monthly, and annual expenses. I mean *everything*, from the house payment to the grocery bill to the property taxes to the green fees for a golf course or tickets to a wrestling match. You just might be surprised as how it all adds up. With this new knowledge (kept private of course) check out the income offered by your career choice. Don't immediately factor in raises or the benefits of a second income when married (another potential financial trap). How does it match up? If it does not match up to your liking, you may want to reevaluate your career choice.

Preventing Financial Turmoil for those over 16

Be patient. It used to be that parents would say that they wanted their children to have a better home and/or lifestyle than they did. By the time the children reached 40 or 50, they had surpassed the standard of living of that shared by their parents. Today, however, we children seem to want to surpass all that our parents achieved in a lifetime within two to three years of being married or settling into a career. The world has responded to our impatience by offering credit at every corner. Many people think nothing of plunging into huge debt to get the things they want now. "Why wait? You deserve it!" screams the commercial. Instant gratification. The only problem is that we now have to focus our efforts on paying off old debt instead of building for the future. Almost out of debt a few years later, another item we must have comes into view, so we take on the financial hot potato again.

Putting off the purchase of certain items can make a monumental impact on your financial well being. Sure, it would be nice to have the larger house, but what about the peace of knowing that if one of you lost your job (if married) the house payment could still be met. Put purchases on a schedule (after you achieve a certain level of savings) or as a reward (we will buy that floor covering when the car is paid off). Those items now become icons for your hard work instead of hitching posts that limit your freedom.

If you want your neighbor's lifestyle, the debt comes with it. With the easy credit today, it has become even more popular to keep up with the... Joneses (they, however, have it as a *last* name). Recently, while helping an 18-year-old landscape a yard, I was amused by his perception of the family that lived in the home. "The husband must make a killing," he said. "Why do you say that?" I asked. "Well, the wife stays at home, they have two nice cars, two kids and a huge house. They're probably only 35 years old." My comment was, "Yes, and if he was out of work for a month, they would probably lose it all." Our perception of the wealth of another person can be skewed by the mask of hidden debt. I had to laugh at the comments of my young friend when I thought about my own life. My wife does not work outside the home (she decorates cakes and helps me with the business), we have one child and four cars (the newest is five years old...all are paid for). Our house is not large, but is comfortable and meets our needs. Above a house payment we have only the typical bills any family would have. If I were out of work for two or three months, I would put my sanity up against the guy in the huge house any day. Maintaining a lifestyle that keeps up with those around us offers us only the opportunity to inherit their restrictions as well. Suppose the husband decides to take another career path in life. The income may well be less for a year or so while he learns his new occupation. They will likely be forced to sell a car, take out a second mortgage, or make some other sacrifice that will allow them to make the change. If, however, they lived at a level that met their needs and provided savings for the future, the pain of change would be much less. In financial matters, meet *your* needs not the need to be like someone else.

A disclaimer may be in order here. I am not anti-wealth. It is of great joy to me to see people acquire material possessions that make their lives easier, more comfortable, or more pleasing. What I do not enjoy is seeing that acquisition at the sacrifice of their happiness or contentment for the moment. If I had to live with the fear that my company might find me expendable at any moment and that it would literally destroy me financially, I would be dead by now. Some stress is good; too much can kill you. I cannot understand families who say their spouse or children are important but then build a mountain of debt that forces them to work every waking moment to meet their financial obligations. A minister once put it best, "You never stop giving to that which you love." I do not think that meant merely gaining money to provide more lavishly for our families. I think it also meant to give the gift of time and your presence to them as well. In one sense you are sacrificing your family for material gain-children have a hard time understanding later, especially when they are grown up and gone. Maybe then the Joneses can share with you a self help book that you need to buy to get over your grief.

If married, live on one income. This, by far, had to be the best one piece of financial advice we ever received. When first married, Lisa and I were in awe at all the money we were making (yes, we were teachers). We had no college loans to repay or cars to purchase or even a house to buy. We rented a small, two-bedroom home in the community in which we taught and, aside from the regular bills, had no debt. We placed a large percentage of one of our incomes in savings and lived comfortably on the rest.

Near the time we moved to our current location, we purchased a new vehicle (the all-American minivan), as well as a house built in the late 1970's. When financing the home, we based it upon one of our incomes. There were larger homes in the community that we could have purchased, but to do so would have required basing our payments on two incomes. A large portion of the down payment came from the money we had saved during the first two years, in addition to some help from parents.

No, I have not lost my topic. I share that because one of the cardinal mistakes many married couples make today is to get accustomed to two incomes. Their lifestyle is one of great fun because there is so much more than can seemingly be purchased. They can purchase a bigger house, park better cars in the driveway and take more exotic vacations. The problem arises when one spouse wants to make a change. The wife may say one day, "Honey, we're going to have our first child." After she has revived her husband, who passed out in his mashed potatoes, he says, "That's wonderful." He then begins to do the math. "Okay, she'll be out for six weeks. We can take some money out of savings and make it." The blessed event takes place, and the happy family is a model one. At a later evening meal, the wife announces, "Honey, I don't think I want to go back to work. I want to stay home with our baby." This time it takes several minutes to get the gravy from around Dad's eyes when he collapses. His heart is racing as he thinks, "How in the world are we going to make it? We've got to have that extra money for payments." I would not want to be in his shoes as he explains to his wife that she can't stay home because they need the money to pay for that nice sport utility vehicle in the garage or the ski vacation to Colorado.

Another similar situation is a job change. Suppose the wife or husband senses a real desire to begin a new career. Even if both members agree it is a good idea, the stumbling block is often, "How are we going to survive for the first six months or year?" Yes, the family can sell the newer vehicles and replace them with older ones and even move into a smaller house for a while. Vacations can be cut and hobbies minimized. All that takes time and energy and is often a financial nightmare. Turf battles can also erupt over where to cut expenses. One spouse may be partial to keeping the nicer house and reducing everything else. The other spouse may see ditching the house and keeping other things intact. Factor in credit card debt, and the hill just got steeper. Realize, too, that all these things are attempted at a time of great stress in the family. Just as a new baby brings immense responsibilities, a career change normally brings enormous stress. Combine these with the desire to downsize your lifestyle, and a recipe for disaster is brewing.

You may have sensed that my foot is slipping onto the ol' soap box again. I am fighting the urge but don't know if I can hold on much longer. It just seems like couples of the 90's who range in age from 20 to about 40 have lost their financial footing. Material possessions come too quickly at the expense of huge credit lines, and couples get locked into careers that are secure (but may not enjoy) and can provide the financial buoyancy to keep them afloat. They live in fear of something happening in the relationship (sickness, baby, etc.), anything that might add to their money woes. Ironically, they really want to be good parents and spouses but must sacrifice those values to avoid financial disaster.

In July, 1994, I went full time into public speaking. The income, however, was not full time. Lisa had been most gracious in telling me that she would continue to work for five years while the business got on its feet. Her one income would sustain us because our self-regulation over the past few years. In late September we found out we were expecting our first child. Those around us gasped: "How will they ever make it? A new baby on the way and Jones just starting a business. This should be interesting." I really do not remember any change in our financial lifestyle. When the baby arrived, I filled in for Lisa at her school for four months while she stayed home with Alex. Then she returned to work while I worked out of a home office and provided care for Alex. After three years the success of the business allowed Lisa to come home, and we now continue to live on an income comparable to what she made in teaching.

Those are not the comments of someone bragging. There were tense moments along the way, but not frequent ones. The joy of spending such an inordinate amount of time with Alex and Lisa went far beyond the smell of a new vehicle or larger home or expensive hobbies or vacations. Limiting our lifestyle to one that was based on a single income gave us flexibility and freedom that we find in few couples our age.

Watch the nickel and dime stuff. Lisa and I are truly a couple of the 90's in that we are credit card users. We have one personal card and one for our business. Based on the mail we get, I do believe we could have fifty each in one month. Rarely do we pay cash or write a check unless it is for incidental items or time to cut back (discussed later). When the bill arrives, Lisa will hesitatingly say, "How bad is it this month?" One month, after telling her the amount on our personal card, she shrieked, "What did we buy?" Handing her the bill, she painstakingly went over it. Finding me later, she said, "I never dreamed $10 here and $15 there could add up to so much." It turned out that *Wal-Mart* had been the source of much of our charges that month. No particularly large items, but simply stuff like motor oil, housewares and a few clothes. They all add up.

When attempting to avoid financial difficulty, watch the small stuff. While we feel good about not making any major purchases in a given time period, the little ones may add up to a similar amount. Forget credit cards for a moment. Take all the cash out of your wallet one day (like there was a whole lot in it in the first place) and go about your normal routine with only a $20 dollar bill or other amount that you believe will sustain you for a given time period. Watch how quickly the money goes away. A raffle ticket here, a cup of coffee there. Then you buy your lunch. On the way home you stop to get a grocery item or two. Soon your cash is spent.

Earlier in the book we looked at the horrors of poor decisions and used the infamous, convenient plastic bottle of soft drink as our point of contention. Although seemingly of little importance, based on an average cost of 75 cents each, let's run the numbers. If you purchase 4 a week for 50 weeks (figures in for holidays and days you overslept), those little moments of refreshment cost you $150 dollars last year. Need another? In the rural area where I live there are several small short-order grills. They have good hamburgers and daily specials, and many, many locals eat there. I frequently hear some of these locals talk about a lack of funds. Watching them pull into the grill several times a week at lunch, I do the math. At an average cost of $3.25 for a meal, $1.00 for tea and a tip of 65 cents, that adds up to $ 4.90. Let's say they eat there three times a week for 50 weeks (if they are not there, they are probably somewhere else). Those lunches took about $735 dollars out of their wallet last year. Ouch! That was money that could be spent on a vacation. Money for a home repair or even part of a down payment for a newer vehicle. "But they have to eat somewhere!" you chide. Yes, they must have nourishment. What about a couple sandwiches from home? If they really wanted to get frugal, they could actually get a small cooler and buy soft drinks (on sale) and pack their lunch. We could do the math, but those who fit the description above might get mad at me and stop reading.

If I seem somewhat sarcastic about this topic, I am. Even in college it would infuriate me when I invited a friend to lunch or to go out, and they would reply that they had no money. They would normally go into an extended explanation about increased book costs or a car problem or a phone bill. The next day they would be raving about a new cassette (CDs not on the scene yet) purchased a couple days ago. We will not even run the numbers on those types of purchases. It can really knock you for a loop. Yes, purchases like tapes, bottled soft drinks, and quick meals are all part of life. Too much free use of such things, however, can add up quickly and slowly undermine our purchasing power for other things.

Stop being a statistic. Ever wonder why milk is in the back of the grocery store, or in an area not easily accessible? Think about it. Bread and milk are two staples most frequently purchased in a grocery store. Why are they not near the front? That's so you have to walk by a number of other items that you may have an impulse to purchase. Marketers know how to get you to purchase more than you planned. A major discount store (no names mentioned) has its own brand of soft drinks in a machine in front of their store for around 35 cents. Name brands are around 45 cents. At the checkout aisle, however, those same name brands in bottles are sold at a much higher rate per ounce. It would seem reasonable that most people would want to save several cents and get their drink outside. Watch the next time you go there (I bet you've been there recently). People, while standing in line, will begin to glance at the cooler. In a few moments the hand reaches out and, taaaaadaaaa! Another consumer marketing strategist gets his bonus for being right.

Fast-food restaurants offer combos that include fries and a drink. You may have entered the place wanting only a sandwich and water, but since the combo is just a dollar more you rationalize that it must be the way to go since it would be cheaper than buying them separately. Wait a minute. I thought you only wanted a sandwich in the first place. Marketing strikes again. Commercials also scream at us to purchase items. As Calvin of *Calvin and Hobbes* fame once said, "Watching TV is great. It makes me want things I never knew I couldn't live without." Even our daughter, who at two-and-a-half-years old watches very little regular TV (Public TV takes precedent), has learned several items that are a must for her collection. She will see them in a store and begin repeating the jingle associated with the product.

When you go into the grocery store, have your list in hand to prevent impulse buying. As the old adage goes, "Do not enter on an empty stomach." Too many grocery stores have bakeries that will literally cause an empty stomach to jump for joy. When you shop in other stores, have a clear idea of what you are shopping for or the total amount you want to spend. Being too open minded can open your mind up to purchases that are less than intelligent.

Do a reality check before a major purchase. You will have to choose the dollar amount here. My wife would tell you that a major purchase for me is anything over $5.00. Doesn't everybody think that way? My reality check consists of three questions: Do I really need it?, Can I borrow it? or will someone give it to me for Christmas? On a more serious (and intelligent) level, ask yourself these questions before taking the plunge on a major purchase:

How often will I use it?   *Is it a necessity?*
Can I do without it?   *Is it the best buy?*
Will it require costly upkeep?
Will it enhance our family relationship?
By investing this money here, what will it take away from other
    purchasing opportunities?

A new car may seem like a grand idea, but if it will cause you to have to work overtime for a while to pay for it, is it worth the strain on your family who will be at home (or somewhere else) without you. My dad must have asked himself these questions when I was about ten. I wanted a horse. It just seemed reasonable to me that we could have one in the field out back. When asked why I wanted one, I responded, "Because I want one to ride." I got a ten speed bike instead. The upkeep was phenomenally less.

Those questions, as pertinent as they may be, must also be asked at the *right* time. Standing in front of a real estate agent or car salesman or stock broker is not the place. While in college, I worked in a jewelry store to make some extra spending money and got the biggest chuckle from people shopping for jewelry. They would try an item on, ask me how it looked, and then think out loud. They would even go so far as to ask themselves questions similar to those listed above. Since I did not work on commission, I would not push a sale and actually found that it built a trust between customer and salesperson that went far beyond the bottom line (many times the customer would return and buy it because I did not force them on the issue). As you have probably discerned from your own life experiences, most salespeople do not operate that way. They will find an answer to your question that favorably influences the purchasing of the product or service they are selling. They move quickly to grab you in the moment of emotion, before reason surfaces in your mind. If you have ever been called by a credit card company, your head is wagging or nodding up and down. "Congratulations, you are pre-approved for a platinum level card with a $ 5,000 limit. All I need to do is to confirm your address and ask a few questions." You almost hate to stop them because they seem to have your best interest at heart. Right. And they would pay your bill if something happened to you one month, too.

If you're married, the advice of a spouse is invaluable. If we are searching for a stamp of approval in every instance, however, we may not feel that way. Spouses often bring up scenarios or questions we had not even dreamed about. Earlier this year I was struggling with the decision to purchase a laptop computer. It just seemed like a huge investment for something that would have marginal use when travelling. When Lisa and I discussed it, she had an entirely different perspective. Her thought was that if I had a portable computer I could complete some of my tasks on the road while in airports, hotels, and similar places. Doing so would allow me to have more quality time to spend with her and Alex when at home. That got my attention. She additionally indicated that a laptop would be great in that I could work away from home, allowing us the flexibility of spending more time with our parents, who live in another part of the state. We purchased one within three weeks. I could cite numerous other instances, but you get the picture. The key is we have to be in the type of marriage that looks out for the other person's needs instead of always our own. We will discuss that further in the nuptials chapter.

Create a cushion. Lisa and I have a set level that our credit card charge can accumulate to each month (it is not the maximum for the card, either). We also have a minimum level for our working savings account (working in the sense that we take out and put in frequently). If either of these two amounts are crossed, sirens wail, red lights flash, and our lives shut down. Well, it's not quite that dramatic. But we do sound a mental alarm and switch to a "back up" system. We will begin paying cash for our purchases. We begin to operate on the premise of "What purchases can we defer for the next few weeks?" Once we have things stabilized, we return to our normal system.

Our reasoning works for us. If we keep a cushion on both ends (savings and spending), we will be prepared for the unexpected. If we need cash to pay bills for three months, it's there. If we need to make an emergency purchase (our freezer dies), we can still make it without borrowing the money from "Mr. Loan Shark" or putting our credit card to such a high level that we will wind up paying those wonderful finance charges. We have rolled coins, had yard sales, and done yard work for other people just to have a few extra dollars in time of need. If we walk the tightrope of having only money for the moment or living in fear that our credit card charges will literally eat our lunch (possibly dinner and breakfast) for the next month, we find that we can not focus on being effective in our roles as spouses, parents, and friends to others.

Credit cards can be your friend. As I said earlier, Lisa and I are religious credit card users. We accumulate frequent flyer points, so there is a motivation to use it for more than just easy payment. As stated earlier, we do have a self-imposed limit on it. I say "it," because that is the only card we have for our personal use.

When I was getting a card for our business with the same company, I was flustered to learn that because of the high limit on our personal card, I could not get a similar one with my business card. At first the low limit on my business card seemed like the biggest pain, but I have found it to be a great asset now. This low amount serves as a limit to what I can purchase in one month. The limit forces me to plan my purchase of plane tickets and office supplies more carefully. Sure I could use the personal card in an emergency, but I have only used it once in the period of one year (when purchasing laptop computer).

If credit card addiction scares you, try getting one card with a low limit. The key is getting just one. My neighbor recently told me of his shock at his credit report. His wife, being a smart lady, had signed up for numerous credit cards to get the free toaster or gift certificate or whatever they were offering. She would immediately destroy the card when getting it and thought no more of it. Guess what shows up on your credit report? Right. All those credit card applications. Granted, no charges were made on them, but it can still be a scary sight to a loan officer. Avoid the temptation to carry extra cards. If you think you might have an emergency, look for a free one as a result of your savings at a bank, or get a check card. They look just like a credit card and function the same way, except that they immediately deduct the amount from your checking account.

Also try to avoid carrying a balance. One radio news report said that the average American family would carry a credit card balance of $4000 into 1998. Lisa and I have never, in our seven years with credit cards, carried a balance. There were months when we had no clue how we were going to pay the bill, but found a way in order to prevent future headaches. The biggest reason we choose to not carry a balance is that doing it once makes it easier. The first time would be difficult, the next would be uncomfortable, and the third time would be convenient. We become desensitized to living on the edge and just think it is normal. Paying someone 13 to 18 percent interest on purchases, which may or may not have been necessary, does not seem like rational thinking to me.

Pay yourself. No matter how small the amount, pay yourself something toward retirement every time you get a paycheck. Even 50 dollars per month is a place to start. Have it payroll deducted if possible to avoid even having the money in your possession. I say that for more than just building a nest egg for your twilight years. If that money is put in the proper place when times are good, then you have some sort of access to it when times are bad. Any financial planner will tell you that it is not a smart move to borrow from your retirement, but most of their loan provisions are much easier to swallow than a second mortgage or debt consolidation. You would only access the money in the event of a dire emergency anyway. Next to someone telling us to live off one income, this was the most powerful piece of advice shared with us in our early years.

Thoughts for those who are currently financially challenged

Seek Professional Help! Remember near the beginning of this chapter when I reminded you that I am not a professional financial planner? The thoughts contained here are simply that... thoughts. Sharing these ideas may help as you encounter specific situations in your own life. They are not offered as absolutes, and should not be taken wholesale. The one thing I would scream at someone and say, however, is to get professional help if you are drowning in a sea of debt. Ask a friend about a financial planner they trust, or consult the yellow pages if you must, but find someone who works with this kind of situation on a regular basis. You may feel embarrassed now, but it will be even more degrading later when your vehicles are traded for much different ones, your house is up for sale, and your friends see you at the courthouse filing for bankruptcy. In most cases, their services are free. Their money is made from getting you into one of their savings vehicles or debt consolidation plans. Talk to two or three financial planners about your predicament.

My first experience with a financial planner was not completely positive. He was competent but really shared no information that I did not already know. The second one, however, was outstanding. Cliff genuinely wanted to help people achieve financial success. He was so powerful in his approach that for a while I thought I wanted to be one. Travelling with him was incredible. He would sit down with a family that seemingly had nowhere to turn, and by the time we left a couple of hours later he had outlined a plan for them that would have them out of much of their debt in two or three years (not including house mortgage). He would ask those probing questions about their spending habits and financial philosophy without the judgmental nature often associated with family members or friends. Those closest to us in life often want to give answers that do not hurt our feelings or make them appear like a villain. Financial planners are removed from those restraints and most likely will tell you the raw facts. What really impressed me was that if Cliff could not help them with an actual investment, he would tell them. There were a multitude of investments or policies he could have forced upon them to make the trip worth his while, but he chose not to pursue them. Almost always, he would get a call from them later when their life had stabilized and financial situation more favorable to his assistance. Cliff would then work with them on a plan that fit their budget and long-term goals. Do your homework, and find a professional to talk with.

Sacrifice, Sacrifice, Sacrifice. If the financial tightrope is fraying, shed some financial pounds. Ask yourself, "What can we get rid of and still function as a family?" Cable TV, extra cell phones, eating out, entertainment, hobbies, or value-added foods at the grocery store are just a few examples of places to cut. One couple, wanting to keep the wife at home with the new baby, told me their attitude was, "What else can we sell to keep our child in the care of mom?" Another couple in the same community had an entirely different attitude. They were a two-car family with one car on its last legs. It needed new tires immediately and a host of other things later. Having heard the couple reveal their financial woes earlier, I was literally floored to hear that the husband had gone to a car race (tickets about $75) and purchased headphones to hear the race (a special kind with a cost of about $200). Excuse me, but where was his brain? He was simply not willing to sacrifice to improve his situation. When people relate their financial difficulties to me, my first thought is always to think about their lifestyle. If I hear about eating out two or three times a week, attendance at expensive sporting events or hobbies which are costly, I have a difficult time feeling sorry for them. "But I need those hobbies or outlets to keep my sanity," you say. An occasional treat, yes. But don't hide behind an unwillingness to sacrifice when tackling financial problems in your life.

Pay the debts with highest interest first. Most likely that will be credit card charges. No matter how much you try to cut back, a finance charge of 13 to 18 percent can quickly erase your other attempts to reduce your outflow of income.

Budget. Any manual on financial well being discusses it.

A Final Thought

If your financial picture is not headed in the direction you most desire, seek help. There are too many self-help books on managing your money or getting out of debt for you to just sit there and have a pity party (charged to your eighth credit card). The answers are not often easy, and averting sure financial disaster may take years of careful planning and commitment. As with any recovery program, the sooner you start, the better.

Finally, let me finish where I began. I am no expert on managing your money and am by no means above the financial strains experienced by many of my friends. In the spirit of getting the most out of life, however, I can honestly say that finances have rarely played a significant role in determining my choice of direction or that of our family life. Having the freedom to choose a path that matches my passions means the world to me. Ask yourself the question, "Are my steps being chosen for me because of my financial decisions, or are my financial decisions allowing me to take the steps desired to a more fulfilling life?" If the answer is the former, find help and get started on the road to recovery. If the answer is the latter, congratulations, and share your words with those around you who need to hear them.

N

Nuptials

First, let me welcome the male readers of this book to the end of *Prime Rib or Potted Meat?* I say that because no doubt if you took my advice and flipped through the book to choose the chapter most applicable to you, you probably avoided this one until the very end. Too "touchy feely" for men. We will discuss that more in the xy chapter later (or you are already in touch because you chose that one earlier).

I sincerely believe that as most people attempt to get the most out of their time on earth many overlook the power of a positive marriage. Beyond a spirituality in your life (see zeal chapter), the support offered by an intimate relationship with your spouse is invaluable. Attempting to put it into words only diminishes its significance. Of course, there are the usual jokes about marriage and the "other" person. My personal favorite goes like this: An elderly married couple were sitting on their front porch one evening. Ethel looked at Fred and said, "Fred, do you remember what my daddy said to you the first time he caught us making out on the porch?" "Yeah, I do," Fred responded. "He said that if I did not marry you, I would have to go to prison for fifty years." They sat in the cool of the evening for a few more minutes, and Ethel noticed that Fred had begun softly sobbing while sitting in his rocking chair. Touched by his seeming compassion, Ethel said, "Oh Fred, that's so sweet. Your memories of our marriage are bringing tears of joy, aren't they?" "No," came his broken reply, "I was thinking that if I had chosen prison I would be a free man by now." I really believe that some people view marriage in just that light. It seems like a confinement, a prison of sorts that limits their ability to obtain the finer things (professional or personal) in life.

Since marriage is different for every person, it would be a waste of your reading time to attempt to list all the benefits of the relationship here. There are other books that can do a better job than my passing thoughts. Instead, let me simply share a few key ways my own marriage has benefited my quest for the best life has to offer.

1) A permanent best friend. Because of our mobile society, the idea of best friends for life has become strained at best. We live in different cities and find our lives filled with responsibilities in our immediate roles (spouse, parent, employee), leaving little time for seeing our dear friends. Even if the relationship is often rekindled by phone calls, visits, or letters, it is just not the same as being together for long periods of time, the foundation that probably built the relationship in the first place.

In my wife I found a best friend for life. I cannot think of anything that I could not talk about with Lisa and vice versa. I never have to wait until I see someone a few weeks later or hope to bump into an old friend who can understand the real me. She knows when to hold and when to scold like only a dear friend can.

2) A shepherd's hook. My wife has rescued me from more than one treacherous situation. During a recent church project, I had the responsibility of developing some promotional materials. I procrastinated until the last minute, of course, and knew that I was in trouble. Not wanting to burden her with my problem, I said nothing to her. After returning from a recent speaking engagement, I was shocked to find all the materials completed and ready for use. Lisa knew what I needed without asking, and completed the task for me, helping me to maintain my sanity and prevent a project from failing.

3) A cattle prod. For those of you who are livestock challenged, a cattle prod is a device (it may or not be electrical) that encourages livestock to move in a direction that is in their best interest. When I was thinking about leaving teaching to pursue a career in public speaking, I was the biggest advocate for making the switch. It was my wife who kept encouraging me to go for it. That may not seem like a major item until you look at the impact of a yes decision. She would become the sole breadwinner for a few years (she gave me five) and would have to put up with all the jokes about a stay-at-home husband. Later, when Alex arrived on the scene, she made the sacrifice to return to work to support us while our business was reaching a sustainable level. She prodded me to be my best and reach for the stars, even if it meant she would have to sacrifice.

4) *A sounding board.* I am amazed at the number of spouses who will tell a friend or relative something but never share it with their spouse. When I ask them why, they will respond, "I couldn't tell them that. It would scare them to death if they knew I thought that." In my marriage, it would scare one of us to death if anyone other than the spouse knew our innermost thoughts before the other. Granted, if you have an abusive spouse, it may not be a good idea to say things to them that would reflect negatively on who they are. However, in most successful marriages I see, it is this sharing of our deepest thoughts and crazy ideas that draw people closer together.

5) *A shoulder to cry on.* This one is especially pertinent to me. Women are usually expected to go to the man to seek comfort when downtrodden. Men, on the other hand, use it as a last resort. They will tell a friend, take it out on something, or just harbor it inside until it comes screaming out in the form of misplaced anger or rage. I can not tell you the number of times Lisa has reached for the tissues as I have shared everything from job disappointments to the loss of a close friend. The old adage that "Tears are a sign of weakness" is a misrepresentation to me. In my opinion, tears are a sign of strength because they show that we are not afraid (which is a weakness) to show our true feelings. It shows that we believe so strongly in the relationship that we are not afraid of how we appear to the other person.

6) *Source of spiritual growth.* Lisa will be the first to tell you that she is no biblical scholar (neither am I). However, her desire to develop a deeper spiritual faith is a model for me and encourages me to examine and strengthen my own beliefs.

By now you are probably thinking to yourself, "Fine, Jones. You're in a great marriage. What does all that mean to me in my plan to get more out of life?" If I stopped at this point, it would mean little. From this point we will broaden our focus to include the strategies for beginning a successful marriage and maintaining spousal happiness.

Beginning a successful marriage

Try to date only those individuals whom you might one day consider marrying. This sounds corny and, no, I did not always follow it, but having worked with so many young people, I am convinced it works. People will say, "Oh, we're just going out once." Something happens that evening, and you decide that you would like to go out with them again. Harmless enough, right? Wrong. Soon you find yourself in a steady relationship with a person who has very different opinions about life and may have some tendencies you really do not like. You stay with that person, however, because the emotional tie tells you that it's okay... they will change and/or you will change them. Maybe, maybe not. All the while you are building a strong emotional and intimate bond that is not easily broken by the intellect or logical reason.

Date someone with similar values. This cannot be stressed enough. Although you may have differences of opinion on some issues, thoughts on religion, sex, abortion, and a host of other issues that may one day enter a marriage do need to be similar. Granted, you do not discuss them on the first date, but they should be discussed before the emotional bond is such that they seem trivial in comparison to the passion of the moment.

Watch what they do, not just what they say. I was extremely fortunate to find someone who had a deep respect for the well being of her parents, because I feel the same way about mine. Just hearing her say it, however, did not prove it to me. Watching her in her relationship with her parents let me know that she really meant it and that she would respond in a similar way with my parents.

Ask yourself, "Am I a better person because of the relationship?" I must credit my mother with this question. When I first told her about dating Lisa, she told me that as long as the relationship made me a better person, she was excited for me. That had great meaning to me because I will never forget one of my relationships in high school that did *not* make me a better person. The girl I was dating was a frequent user of profanity (so was her family), and I picked up the habit without realizing it. One day on the phone my mother heard me utter a couple four letter words, and I quickly received the verbal lashing I deserved. If a relationship brings out the best qualities in us, then it must have potential to end in matrimony.

If you are changing, examine your reasons for changing who you are. Is it simply because you do not want to lose the affection of the other person, or do you really like the person you are evolving into because of the relationship? If it is merely to please the other person, you are cheating yourself and the other person because your old self will one day resurface. Unfortunately, it may be after you are married.

Ask yourself, "What will this person and I do together for fun?" I hear many of you laughing about the honeymoon and the early married years. Okay, okay, I get the joke. But seriously, what common interests do you share or *will* you share in the future? I have a friend whose only common interest with his wife is the college sports team they pull for on game day. Other than that they watch TV, go out and eat, and go on an occasional vacation. Now their common interest is their two children. What will it be later? My wife and I recently asked them about babysitting for their children so they could go out for the evening. Their response was, "Why would we want to do that?" Oh, I don't know...perhaps to rekindle some passion in their relationship and to focus their attention on each other for a change. Silly me, dumb idea. Their children are now two and six months, and they are yet to leave them to enjoy an evening alone.

Lisa and I have a multitude of common interests. We enjoy landscaping, meeting other people, travelling, eating chocolate, fishing, and a world of other past-times. I have found that it is in those times that we share more of our philosophical side and our true selves. Our deep conversations are not relegated to pillow talk, meal time or while watching TV.

Read, Listen, and Ask. Do your homework about the components of a successful marriage before you take the plunge. You would not take a job without knowing its expectations or responsibilities, would you? Some people go to college four or more years to learn skills for a job they may hold for a year or less. What does that say about a job that will last a lifetime, because a positive marriage definitely takes work.

Now if you have already taken the plunge but feel like you are drowning, try these thoughts:

Seek professional help! If you are sick, you go to the doctor. If your roof leaks, you call a carpenter. If you have bugs, you call an exterminator. Why is it that if we have serious marital problems, we just sit around and hope things will get better. If at all possible, involve your spouse in whatever route you choose to improve the relationship. Read the same book, go to the same conference, or talk to the same couple. There are as many different opinions about building a happy marriage as there are places to spend your money. Working off the same opinions or ideas will serve to keep you both on the same plane of thought.

Stop washing the windshield if the car won't run. Ever notice how you get upset with your spouse at the most trivial things? Leaving items out of place, being ten minutes late for something, or even not replacing the toilet paper roll are matches that ignite countless arguments. Unfortunately, there is usually a much deeper problem that rarely gets expressed in a loving tone but instead is used as a weapon to win in an intense argument. Look for the deeper reasons behind your anger or disappointment and seek to express those concerns instead of reminding your spouse about the importance of replacing the cap on the toothpaste.

Reexamine your priorities. Next to my spiritual faith, my relationship with my wife is the most important priority in my life. My parents are extremely important to me, and I know that by taking care of Lisa and meeting her needs she will help me with my parents any way she possibly can. The situation with our daughter is a similar one. Alex is the sweetest little girl on earth, but putting her between Lisa and me only causes a tug of war in which there are no winners. Keeping Lisa first in my earthly relationships insures that Alex will have a mother who is confident and secure, one who has an outlook on life that is not tainted by a weak marital relationship. If your spouse is not a high priority in your life, do not expect your needs to be a high priority in theirs either.

What did I do for my spouse today? Put this question at the top page of your daily calendar or on your sun visor in the car. Some days I get so busy that the only thing I have done for Lisa is tell her I love her when I went out the door. That may be enough to sustain her for a few days, but why not have the conscious desire to do things for your spouse on a regular basis. Sometimes Lisa will begin washing a load of clothes and get busy with another activity. If I hear the washing machine turn off, I get the clothes out, hang them up, and take the rest out to the clothesline or put them in the dryer. Without ever saying a word, I go right back to work. That night before we retire, she will proclaim, "Oh, my goodness, I forgot the clothes!" and scurry to the washing machine. Moments later she will return to the living room with a big smile on her face.

Society has taught us that gifts, romance, and/or being a martyr in our careers are the appropriate ways to show someone we care deeply about them. "I am working hard to provide for you," says the husband. Too bad he's been too busy to notice that she really needs some relief from the children or that she has her own job frustrations that need to be heard. For me, I prefer letting my spouse know that I am in touch with her life by doing those little things that are unexpected. Yes, I do give Lisa cards, flowers, and other appropriate items, but it's the other things I do that seem to make the most difference in how we get along.

Lest I should sound like this is all one sided, Lisa taught me much about this kind of giving. I often get a gift from her that I may have merely mentioned something about months before. She was listening, though, and when I open that gift I know even more just how much she values me because she takes the time to know me. I normally do most of my own ironing, but sometimes I go to the closet and find an army of clean white shirts all neatly pressed. Lisa hates ironing but does it anyway to show that she loves me.

One speaker put it best when he said, "We drift toward isolation, but grow toward intimacy." Marriage is hard work, and taking it easy, putting our energies in other areas of our life, will serve only to drive a wedge between two people that is not easily removed.

One last piece of cake (wedding cake... my favorite kind)

Including marriage as an area to look at to get more out of life may seem odd, but when you consider the implications of a poorly planned marriage (I do not mean the color of the bridesmaid's dresses) or a lazy marriage, it becomes much clearer. Aside from the financial ruin that can occur from a divorce, mental and emotional scars can linger forever, even if a divorce never materializes. All the heartache and mental anguish serve to drain from us the energy and motivation needed to help us reach our loftiest goals and dreams.

On the other hand, a loving relationship built on trust and self-sacrifice cannot only bring us joy beyond compare, it can be one of our strongest resources in times of trouble, frustration, or disappointment. I am the number one fan in my wife's fan club, and I think she is number one in mine as well.

O

Optical Illusions (Perceptions)

Highway 601 runs near our home. (Well, it actually does not run. It basically lies there while people drive across it). It has an odd shape in that at one point it will look like it is clear to pass. Upon pulling out, however, one realizes that the slight twist in the road, combined with the position of the car in front, can hide a car that is actually very close. More than once I have almost caused an accident attempting to pass a slow-moving car in that area, only to duck back into my lane quickly to avoid a speeding motorist coming in the other direction.

The bend in the road is an illusion. Something that appears to be one thing but is actually something very different. One fad that reached its peak about a year ago involved an optical illusion. There were these posters at malls or card shops that at first glance seemed to be some bizarre pattern of colored shapes and figures. If you placed it close to your eyes, however, and attempted to see through the picture, a distinct three-dimensional object would emerge as you moved it away from your face. People are a type of illusion. We think we know who they are but are often fooled by what is revealed in a conversation with the person or from someone who truly knows them. Sometimes it can be very humorous to watch or even to participate in the illusion.

A new pastor in a church wanted to test the compassion of the members of the congregation. He had received letters about how loving the congregation was, that they never met a stranger. Everyone was made to feel welcome at their church. On the morning of the pastor's first Sunday he called and informed them that he would be late, but for the associate pastor to continue with the preliminaries of the worship service, and he would arrive in time for the sermon. He then donned a smelly worn-out trench coat. Before entering the sanctuary he splashed some alcohol on the coat. Armed with a two-day's beard growth on his face and a hat, he took his place on a pew. Not a single individual spoke to him. He could hear murmuring from the others about how he should not come into church drunk or without cleaning up first. Soon it was time for the sermon, and the associate pastor appeared visibly nervous as he thought he might have to preach. While he apologized on behalf of the new minister, the "drunk" stood up and said, "Don't worry, your pastor is here." A tense laugh filled the sanctuary as the faithful thought the old man had had too much to drink. That was until the pastor took off his trench coat and hat to reveal his true identity. I would have loved to have heard the second sermon that day. His illusion had already preached the first one.

Even I have been guilty of misjudging people, if you can believe that. Several years ago while fairly new in the speaking profession, I was asked to address a group of high school students about the dangers of drugs and alcohol. They wanted me to talk about the power of being positive about who you are and about being a role model for others as well. As I came in, I did as I normally do and talked with the students. One young lady summoned me and said, "Mr. Loflin, I want you to meet Jeremy." Let me describe Jeremy. He was wearing a worn-out blue T-shirt, bell bottom jeans with multiple holes, and a pair of Chuck Taylor Converse tennis shoes. His hair was untidy at best, and he had a glare on his face that immediately announced I was not welcome in his world. I politely said, "Hello Jeremy, it's nice to meet you." Lying, of course. He simply responded, "Yeah, same here," and returned to talking with his friends. The young lady, however, wanted to continue our happy (tongue in cheek) gathering. She said, "Jeremy, why don't you show Mr. Loflin your tattoo?" Jeremy sheepishly smiled and turned his back and proceeded to tug at the back of his pants. "Oh, my goodness!" I thought. "I can see the headlines now. Speaker at local high school caught staring at student's posterior." Fortunately, his hands were reaching for his shirt tucked into his pants. He then pulled up his shirt to reveal a tattoo that covered his entire back. It looked like a naked man with multiple arms and a circle around it. I immediately said, "Nice tattoo" (another lie), and headed to the stage for my program.

If you have ever heard me speak, you know that I like to use audience volunteers in my programs. Nearing my last few points of the keynote, I asked for another volunteer. For some reason, the only hand raised was Jeremy's. Having no choice but to bring him on stage, I did so and began the activity. I threw in a couple of cute but pointed comments about his pants and tried to get his cooperation for the activity. Jeremy, however, sensing my disdain for his appearance, had other ideas. He poked fun at what we were doing, and deliberately tried to goof up the point I was attempting to make with his help. I finally finished the activity and got him back to his seat. As I finished the program, I was furious. Everything had gone so well until he got involved. While walking around the courtyard at lunch and talking with the students, I spied Jeremy sitting all alone at a picnic table. Revenge on my mind, I sauntered over to him, planning to annihilate him with a few cutting remarks. As I approached him, I said, "Hey, Jeremy, where are all your friends?" Granted, it's an old line, but the point was still made. Jeremy responded, "They're still in line in the cafeteria." "Didn't you eat?," I asked. "Yes," came his quick reply. "How did you get through the line so quickly?" "I was in a line serving different food." Not wanting to lose the opportunity to "slam" him about something, I asked, "What did you have for lunch?" "Vegetables and water," came his quick reply. At this point I may need to clarify something for the non-parents in our audience. High school students avoid vegetables like I avoid speeding tickets. As for water, that sounded a bit strange, too. "Why vegetables?" His response floored me. "Mr. Loflin, the way I figure it, we have to put good stuff in our body if we want to feel good. My friends eat food high in fat and sugar. They drink caffeinated drinks before coming to school to get a kick to stay awake. They crash by fourth period unless they get a candy bar or something else to push them back up." Astonished by his wisdom, I said, "Tell me more."

"If you get a kick from caffeine in soft drinks, you may be tempted to try smoking to check out the boost of nicotine. Soon it may be beer or marijuana. The cycle never ends. My thought is that if we put only good things in our body, we will get mostly good things out." Then he pointed to his back and said, "That's what my tattoo is all about." Really intrigued by all this, I asked to see it again. He raised his shirt to reveal the large purplish image. In the bright sunlight I could now see the sketch found in many doctor offices and on medical signs. It is of a man with arms in several positions, with lines behind it. It is some type of ancient symbol for good health. Now you can argue all you want about the unhealthiness of a tattoo and the poor choice of getting one. That thought is secondary in importance here.

In case you have forgotten, my purpose in talking with the students that day at Jeremy's school was to illustrate the value of having a positive attitude and to tell them how the influence of drugs or alcohol can ruin their chance of a reaching their maximum potential. Here was the poster boy for my program, and I had missed him because of an optical illusion. I saw something that was not as it appeared to be. I immediately said, "Jeremy, I'm sorry. I misjudged you, and I sincerely apologize." Jeremy obviously saw beyond my optical and verbal illusions as he said, "Mr. Loflin, I appreciate what you said today. I really believe that we're reaching for the same things in life. We're just taking different paths to get them." This young man was wise beyond his years.

I think Jeremy's words could be said of many of our relationships. We may be different in our approach but our goals are similar. The horror of misjudging others comes in that they could be partners in our success or we could be instrumental in helping them achieve their dreams. How then can we avoid seeing an attitude or behavior in someone that does not actually exist? Here are some possible strategies:

Remember image is everything.... except the absolute truth. When dating in high school, I went out with a girl who wore a smock over her shirt that strangely resembled the ones worn in a major discount store. That didn't occur to me until we were shopping in that store and she was asked the location of everything from shaving cream to watch batteries. She was very embarrassed, but our clothing really does sometimes give a false impression of who we are.

If you have read my chapter on image, you sense a contradiction developing. No, I don't think the idea of choosing appropriate dress for the right image and then later not accepting one's dress as a total reflection of who they are operate against each other. As we mature in our leadership skills, we realize that wrong appearances can be an immediate turn off and that the best safeguard is to dress at a level that is most expected in our current role or capacity. Other people may not be as aware of their need to be professional and, consequently, send the wrong messages with their words, actions, or even their clothing.

While serving as a state officer of a youth organization, I had the pleasure of working with one young man as a fellow officer. His exuberance for life was matched only by his desire to be a good officer. While at a conference representing our organization, I overheard him repeating some rather off-color jokes by a popular comedian. I later pulled him to the side and said, "What are you doing?" His hollow eyes responded with, "What are you talking about?" He genuinely had no idea. After I explained the importance of not putting down other individuals or groups, he apologized. He even went so far as to talk with those people who heard him earlier and offered his apologies to them as well. Sometimes people have no idea they are presenting themselves in a certain light. Instead of belittling them, give them the benefit of a doubt until an intelligent investigation yields a different answer.

Look for the oak tree in the acorn. When you look at people, do you see the oak tree in the acorn? In other words, do you see them for the long-range value they may have as a friend or business partner, or do you see them as a nut? Something that causes us to stumble and needs to be kicked out of the way? Remember, "If you see yourself as a hammer, you will respond to everyone else as if they were a nail." Even if people appear to be at the opposite end of the spectrum to us, they probably have some sort of intrinsic worth to us in our personal or professional endeavors.

As a first-year teacher, I wanted all my students to sit quietly in their seats, do well on written tests, and follow all my directions. That happened on the first day, but beyond that I had the range from the head of the class to the juvenile who was recently released from prison (no joke). I got a kind of warped pleasure in giving them poor marks on their papers. "I'll show them," I thought. While I had great misgivings about the difficult ones being in my class, I began to find a certain respect for them by the time I began my second year of teaching. Instead of just opening their minds and accepting my words unquestioningly as the academically gifted students did, these hardened individuals would question the validity of my teaching. They would try my technical skills on the anvil of experience. While the class was in a unit on woodworking, one student wanted to attempt a difficult design on a project. Against my better (insecure because I could not do it) judgement, I allowed him to continue. It turned out to be the hit of the class, and almost every student copied his design. The students who at first seemed to be my nightmare became some of my greatest assets.

Whether in a school, an office, or in our communities, there are always people who can teach us much about life if we just give them a chance. My cousin in school taught me a valuable lesson. He was my opposite in many ways. While he made good grades and attempted the difficult classes just as I did, the similarities stopped there. His parents did not get along very well, and he hung around some rather questionable characters. His attitude toward religion was much different than mine, and the list goes on. After graduation he bounced around a few jobs before joining the Air Force. He seemed to enjoy his experiences in the military, and I was glad to see that he had found a clear direction in his life. I feel quite fortunate when I consider how easy my path to this point in my life was compared to his obstacles. It was ironic when we talked a few years ago. He expressed his envy of me, my relationship with my parents, and my chance to go to college. I laughed and told him about my jealousy of his athletic ability, charm with the girls, and high degree of skill in woodworking and mechanical areas. We had both learned a lot from each other and never expressed it.

Put yourself in their situation. It is an old piece of advice but still a sound one. Attempting to see things from the other person's point of view can be a helpful step toward better understanding their actions or attitudes. Recently, an insurance salesman was at our home, getting information for a policy application. When she was asked about her weight, Lisa begrudgingly shared it, along with the comment that she still had not lost the weight from having a child. The man said, "I understand." Lisa laughed and said, "Oh no, you don't!" There are many instances in which we can in no way fully get to another person's way of thinking. Someone attempting suicide used to be something that I thought I would never comprehend. Having worked with students from tough home situations, suffering various inferiority complexes and even mental incapacities, I can now see why some would choose suicide as a permanent solution to a temporary problem. Our ability to empathize with others has its roots in a genuine desire to know the *person*, not the personality. If our goal is merely to pick someone apart for all the things that are distasteful to us, then we will never get past the initial impression and prejudices.

When in doubt, ask. "So now you're saying that I should just walk up and say, 'Hey, are you a great person, or a real jerk?'" That would be okay if you were talking to me but not for the majority of the population. I base this on the fact that most people who really want to know something about someone will do everything but ask them. They will ask their friends, co-workers, and anybody else they can find to get the information. All the while their perceptions of that person are being more firmly etched in mental stone in their minds, possibly damaging the hopes for a positive relationship.

More than once I have been asked if I am a Baptist preacher. "No," comes my reply, "why do you ask? Is it something I said?" Their response normally points to something about my animated nature or my voice inflections and has nothing to do with what I have said. I sincerely appreciate their asking, especially if they return to their local school or youth organization and talk about me. Imagine them planning their annual conference or a high school assembly, and one student exclaims, "Let's get Jones as our speaker!" Another student responds, "He sounded like a Baptist minister," meaning it purely as a descriptive term. Another student says, "Well, we better not get him. You know how it would go over if we had a religious speaker." Because one of the young people had asked, he could explain my background and remove any misconceptions.

If you cannot actually talk with the person or groups involved, ask someone in a similar situation. I grew up in an all white town and rarely had the opportunity to associate with African Americans. When

I entered college, I found a different scenario as I met people of all colors, races, and creeds. Some particulars of the African American culture were strange to me, as I am sure mine were to them. I soon made friends with an African American through a student organization. An added bonus of our friendship was that I could ask him about anything. A standing joke became, "Okay, Jones, what can I tell you about us today?" We shared religious practices, music choice, and a host of other things in the light of better understanding each other.

Listen. If you can get your mind to hold off on printing its final analysis of someone before you hear them talk, do so. Listen for what you hear or do not hear in their words. Teachers can quickly size up the support young people get from home by the way they discuss their parents. Likewise, the strength of a marriage is made relatively plain to me when someone is discussing a job change. Hearing (or not hearing) their concern on how it might affect their spousal relationship is a key indicator.

Over the past several years I have had the opportunity to coordinate several officer training conferences. One advisor I met was a role model for others to follow. Her professionalism and exuberance for her job were incredible. Over the years, however, I sensed a change taking place. She became more critical of her officers and at planning meetings was openly indifferent about a course of action. She even made some rather cutting remarks to me that I considered way out of bounds, but I refrained from attacking her (I was so proud of myself). However, her negative nature had become a point of contention for those around her.

A few months ago I saw her at one of the officer training conferences. In casual conversation, she mentioned that she was tired of all this stuff. I asked what she meant, and then I understood. She was burned out in her current job and just wanted a change. I now understood that her negative comments, though out of place, were just a reflection of a deeper conflict. Listening may not reveal a mother lode of information that opens the individual like a book, but it may uncover some hidden circumstances or challenges facing the individual that begin to explain (not necessarily excuse) their words or actions.

Wrapping It Up

My wife's favorite TV show, now that *Little House on the Prairie* has gone off, is called *Early Edition.* In the show, Gary Hobson, the lead character, gets tomorrow's newspaper today. His days are then spent preventing tragedies and accidents. He will even go so far as to put his own life in danger to save someone else or prevent disaster. People rarely say, "Okay, I understand, I'll see things your way and change course." Instead they argue with him, question his authority, and call him a nut case. My thought is always, "Show them the paper!" but I know they would simply laugh at it. To really prove his point he has to show them the circumstances (i.e. oncoming car, bomb, etc.) of the situation to get them to comply. Real people are similar in nature. We always feel like our perceptions are best and literally have to be beaten over the head with something before we will agree to see things differently. Unfortunately, some people are not as persistent as Gary Hobson and will leave us alone to make the sad mistake of misjudging someone's attitude, character, or values.

Another facet of the show makes it intriguing. As the day goes on, the headlines mysteriously change. If Gary does not continue to look at the paper throughout the day, he misses something that was not even there first thing that morning (the paper arrives at 6:30 AM). Such is our story, too. People are constantly changing creatures. While some of their values remain the same throughout their years, their attitudes and thoughts on life are constantly evolving. For us to assume we know them because of who they *were,* five, three, or even one year ago is shallow at best. Focusing on their value as a person and taking the time to dig below the surface can reduce the possibility for embarrassment, humiliation, or loss of trust. Remember, seeing is not always believing, whether it is a bend in a highway or a person with an odd tattoo.

P

Personality

Clinical studies tells us that there are basically two personality types: A and B. Type A is a focused, intense, goal-oriented individual while Type B tends to be a more laid-back, relaxed person who pretty much takes life as it comes to him. To put it in layman's terms, a Type A person would have read this book in a few hours or over the course of a few days. On the other hand, such a person might not even purchase it at all because at the end of the program they were in a rush to get to another activity or commitment. A Type B individual might buy the book since they were standing around after the program, socializing, and enjoying the camaraderie. Once home, however, they may never have opened the book because too many other things just keep getting in the way. These are exaggerations but give you a basic understanding of the concept.

Problems arise because we rarely fit into one category or another. People are complex individuals who will respond as Type A's in one situation while reflecting Type B characteristics in another. When I clean house, I am more of an A, wanting to get it done as quickly as possible. Lisa will even remark, "Alex, get out of the way. Daddy is in his cleaning mode again, and he might even throw you away." When I read, however, it's a different story. I will read a page, reflect on it, and sometimes even reread it before moving forward. Getting to the end does not interest me as much as just absorbing the information at the moment.

What comes next in this chapter is a somewhat humorous synopsis of six personality characteristics that I think most of us reflect at one time or another. While some of us may strongly exhibit one or two of the characteristics, others may be a conglomeration of three or four. I share them because I believe that understanding someone's personality (or personalities) can go a long way in appreciating their value to your organization or group. Additionally, it helps us evaluate what types of tasks we might best be suited for and which ones would cause us immediate frustration.

Personality Characteristics
The Pencil Eraser

When is the last time you talked about the virtue of a good pencil eraser? Did you spend hours and hours picking out a pencil based on the quality of the eraser? Of course not. A pencil eraser is a pencil eraser, no more, no less. It is designed to remove marks a pencil makes, and that is its only purpose. A pencil-eraser person is someone who likes to work with their hands, machines, tools or small instruments. They would rather work with *things* than with people or ideas, and they like an immediate sense of accomplishment. They function best when given a list of things to be done. In group settings they may tend to focus on details like location, time, etc. Brainstorming is not their favorite activity, and fluffy details do not interest them. Just like a pencil eraser that does not care what words it erases, this type of person wants primarily to just do something.

If you were planning a party using a representative from each of the personality groups, the pencil eraser would want to sign up for putting up decorations (not planning what decorations to use), addressing envelopes, or working in the kitchen. Their desire would be to know the exact time the party was to start, and what time it would be over. They would refrain from taking a leadership role in some cases because their forte is working with things, not people. No, they're not brainless individuals, nor are they antisocial. They just work better with objects. A key phrase they will often use is "Just tell me what you want me to do."

The Microscope

In high school biology I was fascinated with a microscope. I would bring in pond water, strange leaves, and other objects to examine under the lens. Often I saw a completely different makeup or structure in the item that could never be seen by the naked eye. Microscope people are like this. They are usually people who enjoy reading about advancements in science or technology and probably liked math and/or chemistry in high school. In group meetings, they tend to be critical of ideas, not because they do not like what they see, but because they want to think it through before making a decision. They tend to ask "why" much of the time. Microscope people work best when given a problem and asked to come up with a solution. If given a list of things to do, they will analyze each one for a more efficient way of doing it or if it really needs to be done at all.

In regards to party planning, they will want to devise a plan to get as many people there as possible. If parking or traffic flow is going to be a problem, they will jump at the chance to develop a solution. Again, the most common word in their vocabulary is "Why?"

The Piano

One of my greatest failures in life thus far is not taking piano lessons seriously. For nine years I pecked away at the keys, but can only struggle through a church hymn or piece of music of similar difficulty. Looking back, I regret it immensely because I still believe the piano is one of the most expressive musical instruments that exists in our world. One can produce every emotion from despair to utopian joy by choosing just the right combination of keys and pedals. Some people remind me of a piano in the way they conduct themselves. These people like to work in creative, expressive, imaginative areas. Just as a piano offers eighty-eight individual sounds, they tend to offer a multitude of ideas (especially during brainstorming) but later cannot add the specific details (combine the sounds into a beautiful melody). They rarely see answers as wrong and are often moody. Like a piano, they are complicated, and one must be very patient in getting to know them or miss, if not careful, some skill or positive trait. They may take on tasks such as posters but be unable to complete them by a deadline because they keep having great ideas.

In our quest for the ultimate party, they will want to be a part of everything. They will have great ideas on all facets of the party from location to music to food to decorations. They will happily take responsibility for a portion of the party arrangements, but do not be surprised if they bounce around to other groups to offer their wonderful ideas to them as well. A common buzz phrase with piano people is "Let's think about this for a moment," or "Wait! I have a better idea!"

The Seesaw

Since most all of us have ridden this marvelous piece of playground equipment, I will dispense with the descriptors or long explanations. Seesaw people definitely have the attitude that it takes two (or more) to be happy. They like to be in situations to meet new people and help them in some way. In group settings, they will tend to look at the impact on others as the basis for their decision making. They are especially helpful in times of conflict with others because they often serve as peacemakers (preventing someone from jumping off the seesaw and hurting another person). They usually talk more than others and do not see answers as clearly right or wrong.

Seesaw people take an interesting stance when working on our party-planning committee. Working behind the scenes is not their area of desired participation. They want to be in charge of the music or activities of the evening. When discussing the particulars of the party, they will always struggle with what other people will like. Their common phrase is "What would people like to see (or hear or do) most?"

The Bulldozer

My father-in-law works as a supervisor in road construction. Having visited his job sites in several states, I am constantly in awe of what a bulldozer can do. With its mighty steel tracks, it can go up or down seemingly impossible slopes. Tree stumps, most rocks, and other debris are no match for the bulldozer and its blade as it prepares a road bed for smooth travel by others later. Bulldozer people work just the same way as they prepare a path to success for themselves and the group in which they are involved. These people are persuasive, ambitious, confident, assertive. They enjoy organizing projects, promoting things, being leaders, and getting involved. In group settings they tend to take charge of a situation, get people organized, and make decisions quickly. They do not like beauracracy and are often workaholics. They see answers as a means to head in a direction and get things done (show me where you want the road and get out of my way).

As for the party, they are probably the ones leading the meeting (or wishing they were). They want people's ideas to a point but then want to delegate things and get started as soon as possible. They will get frustrated if someone says more information is needed before a decision can be made because they want to act on it now. Bulldozer people will also be the first ones to arrive to help and usually the last ones to leave. Their favorite phrases are "What do we need to do next?" or "Let's plan the best way to do this."

The Calculator

Chemistry was never my favorite subject in high school (and yes, I do not have a microscope personality). I enjoyed the experiments if something smoked, boiled, or made strange odors, but I hated all the equations. If you did not convert this mole to match that mole, then your solution was wrong. Who cared if the moles matched up? The only moles I planned to see after high school were the kind that were related to mice. They lived underground, so I still don't know if they had a similar matching problem. Calculators made Chemistry easier, but even then you had to be careful. If you punched the wrong key or operation sign, your equation would be totally off. To make matters worse, they would even put that absurdly wrong answer as an option on a multiple choice test. It was just not fair.

Calculator people have a plan all their own. They like activities involving precise order. They are usually organized and like thing to fit in neat packages. In group settings they ask for clarification of ideas and suggestions so that they understand them more fully. In tasks, they like lists and want to see things done in a specific order. Calculator people are not usually overly creative and like to do tasks the same way each time.

As a party planner, they will volunteer to work in any area. They typically will want to do things requiring a specific process or repetition (pouring punch or serving food). Calculator people will count the number of chairs to make sure there are enough seats for everyone and also reject any last minute new ideas because they are uncomfortable with changing a process that has worked in the past. Their model comments are, "We have never done it that way before," or "If it's not broke, don't fix it."

Working with Personalities

To maintain the practical nature of this book, we must go further than just identifying typical personality characteristics or types. Bringing them together and getting them to work together is difficult to say the least. You have the bulldozer and the pencil eraser wanting to get on with the business at hand while the calculator and piano people are having a heated debate because one wants to try a new idea while the other believes they should keep things the same. Even the microscope and seesaw people can't see eye to eye because the seesaw person views the critical nature of microscope's comments as an attack on other people. Let's return to our unhappy group, then, and look at ways to get the most out of each person's personality.

The Pencil Eraser. You will have to prod these people often if you want them to make suggestions or give comments. Try to recall their role in a past project and highlight it so they can see the value of what they do. Pencil eraser people are sometimes in the background and do not get the positive strokes of a Seesaw or Bulldozer person. When assigning responsibilities, allow the person to choose their area if possible. Taking them outside their comfort zone (making them a greeter) may not be appropriate, especially if your relationship is relatively new or they are not a seasoned veteran in your organization.

The Microscope. Let this person know (in private) that even though you know they mean nothing by their critical nature, it still inhibits others from suggesting new solutions. Give them tasks that are deductive in nature (looking at all solutions to choose the best one). Remind them that indecision is a decision and that there are cases where they must make a decision and make it right, whether or not the hard facts are in front of them.

The Piano. Help the piano person see the need for structure or order in things. They need to be gently reminded that it would be nice to be able to follow up on all creative ideas, but the expense in money and time resources does not make it possible. If a Piano person is given a task, stay in close contact with them, frequently checking their progress. You may even want to give them a deadline that is premature to your actual deadline, just in case they have a last-minute brilliant idea.

The Seesaw. Working with these people is relatively easy once you get them to be quiet and listen. Help them understand that any decision made will affect some people negatively, and that we sometimes have to choose a direction that is of greatest benefit to the largest number of people (life is not fair). By all means let them fulfill their peacemaker role because it is desperately needed in today's professional and personal climate.

The Bulldozer. While excellent in leadership roles, they may have unrealistic expectations of their peers. Remind them that not everyone is as passionate about things as they are and that others in the group need to use their exuberance but not their antagonistic attitude. Slow them down if you perceive they are moving at a pace that others cannot keep up or understand. Remember, "He who calleth himself a leader, but has no followers has taken a walk in the dark."

The Calculator. Success stories of how your organization or group changed their mode of operation and achieved greater efficiency or impact are a good place to start. The calculator person sees order as their security blanket, and you may have to help them visualize the worst-case scenario if a new direction is taken. Often, once they see that the new procedure or idea will not be the downfall of the free world, they are willing to go along with your plans. If the process can be reversed later, remind them of that and give them a point when they could expect things to return to normal.

Mixing the Salad

Until my college years I had always heard of America as a melting pot where people from all over the world could come and be called an American. It was then that a college professor called America a "Salad Bowl." While we are all in the same geographic location, each person brings his or her own unique traits to it. When properly mixed, they create something that is a joy in which to participate. (I always hated it when professors talked about food in class, especially around noon)

Any organization needs a mixture of all personalities if it is to be successful. The creative suggestions of the Piano may seem ridiculous until the Bulldozer finds a way to make them happen. The chaos of the moment can be calmed by the exacting directions of the Calculator. Some of our greatest discoveries come when people ask "Why?" like a Microscope person would be inclined to do. When things are falling down around us and there seems to be no one to take on the load, the Pencil Erasers teach us all something about loyalty and commitment to a cause. Lastly, the world would be a cruel place without the See Saw people looking out for you and me. The key then becomes helping them appreciate their differences and the value of each entity to the whole.

Q

Quality vs. Quantity Time

A wise old man was once asked the question, "Which is more important in maintaining a relationship...quantity time or quality time?" The guru responded, "What is your favorite dessert?" "Cheesecake" was his quick response. "What, then, is another dessert of which you are fond?" "Well, I really don't have a close second, but chocolate chip cookies are good." The old master then whispered, "Which would you rather have, a plate full of chocolate chip cookies or two bites of cheesecake?" Realizing the futility of his question, the man went off in despair.

The question of quality time versus quantity time quietly surfaces in the minds of almost everyone, from the stay-at-home mom to the rising corporate executive. The common thrust of most self-help books has been that quality time is most important and can do much to make up for a lack of quantity time. Quality time can be defined as time with someone or something that makes the other entity happy, productive, and/or content. Quality time has become the mental medication for a busy world since we have been taught that making the most of the few moments we are together with someone will create harmony in a relationship or increased efficiency in the workplace. The problem with that logic, however, is that it places tremendous pressure on an individual to make that brief time together memorable.

It reminds me of getting ready for the Junior-Senior Prom when we were in high school. We purchase, borrow, or rent nice clothes and order flowers. Girls often have their hair and/or fingernails perfectly prepared. Young men rent limos or borrow their neighbor's fancy sports car or at least wash their own heap before the big evening. Reservations are made at trendy restaurants. Both individuals have done much to insure that their time at the prom is of great quality.

Unfortunately, things quickly unravel. The pouring rain flops the hairstyle, and the guy is upset because all that washing and waxing of the car was useless. It takes over an hour to get served at the restaurant, and they arrive late at the prom. Feeling stressed because of all the expectations for the evening, they look forward to some intimate time dancing and enjoying what time is left. The young lady feels a tap on the shoulder and turns to see her best friend in tears. She learns that her friend is crushed because her date left her for an old flame who came to the prom looking gorgeous. Now the young lady spends an inordinate amount of time consoling her best friend, while the guy is reduced to hanging around the food table drinking punch. If they make it together through the evening, they return to her home, feeling frustrated that a perfect evening has become a perfect nightmare.

Sound familiar? Perhaps you cannot readily relate to the prom experience, but you get my point. Creating extremely high expectations for a period of time is dangerous. Frequently, external events will intrude on your happy time together, leaving one or more individuals feeling unfulfilled and discontent in a relationship. As the opportunity window for having quality time together continues closing, we force ourselves to place even more emphasis on getting the most from the moment, only to be distracted by a ringing phone, crying child, work beeper or any of a hundred circumstances.

On the other hand, just focusing on quantity time does not seem to be our ticket to bliss in a relationship either. Look at young unmarried couples who spend almost every waking moment together. They seem to be on a sure path to matrimony when one exits the relationship because they were bored or just felt like the passion was gone. One married couple in our community recently divorced. As I talked with the husband, his comment was, "Jones, I just don't understand it. I never beat her, treated her bad, or stormed out of the house in anger. I provided for her financially and tried to be a good dad to our child." What was interesting was what I did not hear. In our entire conversation I never sensed that one of his priorities in the marriage was to make her *happy*. Rather, he provided the necessities. Like a bowl of cereal without milk or watermelon without salt (A Jones thing), something was just missing. People work extraordinary hours at a career, only to see it crumble in their hands because they merely spent time there instead of engaging their mental and physical energies.

It is my belief that in order to be successful in our roles as a family member, friend, or employee, we must achieve a balance between quality and quantity time. One without the other creates a situation much like our dear guru described earlier in the beginning. Either will meet a need, but neither satisfies the deep desires or hungers within us.

Family Quality Time

As we have discussed in earlier chapters, families are often sacrificed on the altar of career success because our reasoning is that they will be around when we decide to come home. Sensing the strain in the relationship, the spouse plans a weekend getaway for the family. They rationalize that this quick burst of quality time will overhaul the relationship. The weekend time is great, and fond memories are made. On the drive home, however, conversation drags, and a tenseness fills the vehicle. They know that once they enter the house, their fairy tale weekend is over, and the rat race will begin again. When a time for the next quick-fix weekend rolls around, the excitement seems diminished because they know it will end in a similar way.

Mental injections of instant euphoria from attempts at quality time rarely sustain us for long periods. A few years ago, I traveled much of the year as a national officer for a youth organization. Lisa and I had begun dating, and the strain on the relationship was huge. After a five-week stint on the road, I surprised her by arriving at her dorm room an hour earlier than she anticipated my return. She opened the door, grabbed the flowers I had brought, and we embraced for what seemed like hours. We told the entire world to go away and just spent the time holding hands and catching up on each other's lives. Our hour having expired, I had to leave to make the drive home. Lisa later told me the evening was bittersweet. She was appreciative of my presence, but the fleeting jolt to her emotions was quickly replaced by loneliness as she gazed at the flowers sitting on her desk.

Explain quality time to a young child. Sure, they appreciate it when you walk in the door and immediately hug them and offer to read a book. An hour later, however, when you have stepped back into your own little world, don't expect them to say "Wow, my mom (or dad) is really something. They read to me every evening." Instead, expect them to bring that book to your work area and beat it on your computer keyboard until you read it to them again. Watch for them to capitalize on any opportunity to get your attention. Why? Because children don't understand the difference between quality and quantity time. They only know if you are there or not and what you are doing with them when you are home or in their presence.

At two and a half, Alex has quickly picked up on our stall tactics. When we were extremely busy or engaged in an activity that needs to be finished, we used to tell her, "In a minute." Now she uses that same phrase sometimes when we ask her to do something. She has no clue what a minute is, but she knows that it means she can delay something. As she gets older, she will, of course, learn the meaning of time, but by then she may also have learned that Mommy or Daddy want to spend their quantity time on something else if we do not make her a priority now.

Look back on a relationship with a best friend in high school or college. They became your best friend because you spent many hours together. Engaging in a "quality" five-minute conversation might be stimulating, but it just never draws two people together like a trip to the doughnut shop, going to a movie, or studying biochemistry together. It is in these seemingly low-quality moments that we really get to know the other person and build the emotional bonds necessary to sustain a relationship. The most common phrase I hear people use about their best friends is, "We did everything together."

Determining how we are doing on our balance is not easy. One benchmark for me to use is, "Am I spending enough time with Lisa (quantity) to know what to do to meet her needs and make her happy (quality)?" Have I been in her presence enough to know about her frustrations, disappointments, and achievements? Not just the major ones, but the seemingly small ones as well. Alex does not pose quite as complicated a problem just yet. I can determine my proficiency with her by how much she questions me. "Will you read to me?" or "Can we paint?" or "Will you swing me?" are common survival questions from Alex. Even though I feel guilty when I cannot meet all her requests, I feel relatively safe that if she is asking, then she must have some faith that I will honor my commitments to her. An interesting aside to that is her way of letting Lisa or me know that we will do what she asks. If Lisa is busy at the moment she is summoned by Alex, I may volunteer to assist her with coloring or playing a game. Her aggressive response will normally be, "No! Mommy's going to color with me!" While my feelings are bruised by her momentary exclusion, my heart grows even fonder for my wife because I know that Alex places great trust in what Lisa says she will do with her. When she stops asking me, it will be time to worry, especially as she gets older and searches for that contentment in places that may not contribute positively to her development.

Family Quantity Time

The phrase: "You never stop giving to that which you love" has been used previously in this book. The phrase bears on everything from time management to priorities to relationships. Here it underscores the power of quantity time with our families. If we care about the well being of someone, we will want to spend time with them. Stopping there, however, severely limits our ability to grow in the relationships if a desire for quality is not a prerequisite of that time.

A former member of our community called Lisa and asked about us babysitting their youngest child (they have three under the age of seven). Lisa was not home, so we struck up a conversation about her husband's new job, their house purchase, and other stuff. "John is working fourteen to sixteen hours a day," she said. "Most of the time he comes home after the children go to bed and leaves before they arise in the morning. Recently, though, we got a computer, and he can bring work home so he actually has a physical presence in the house." Bingo! This extremely bright, transplanted Northerner hit the nail on the head. She correctly pinpointed the neurosis plaguing many parental relationships as well as spousal relationships. The physical presence is there (quantity) but not much else.

"Jones, if you had my job, you would understand." I will readily agree that there are many careers out there in which I could not mentally or physically sustain myself. Regardless of the career, however, it seems to be a terrible tragedy when we take our best to work or to our relationships with our friends, leaving only our physical presence home for those we say we love the most. Granted, if your job requires travel away from home, just being in the same house with your loved ones may provide joy for the moment, but without engaging in focused activities with them, one can become a stranger in their own home.

Career Quality/Quantity Time

Although work is a totally different area of concern, our careers can also be made or broken by our balance of quality and quantity time. Simply attempting to throw hours or years of wholesale time at a job may yield little more than an intensely focused "crash course." Neither creates a foundation for career success like a combination of the two.

Since my background is in education, we will use it as our model. It takes approximately four years to become a classroom teacher. One must pass their classes, apply for a teaching certificate, and perhaps student teach under the auspices of a seasoned veteran educator. Those are the quantity requirements, with the four years or so being the quantity time needed. Does that make a successful teacher? Sure, like standing in a garage makes you a car. Just meeting the base requirements means little when you enter the classroom on your own.

However, if you choose to visit teachers of similar subject matter and get advice from them, you are on your way to being a better teacher. If your subject matter is of a technical nature, you may decide to complete an internship in that area or at least work in the industry for a short period of time. Those are the marks of a teacher focused on quality, one who will likely do a much better job shaping the lives of young people.

Taking the example a step further, watch two very different educators as they carry out their daily responsibilities. Mr. Quantity will arrive at the same time as Ms. Quality. They teach the same subject and have the same amount of time with their students. The students in Ms. Quality's room seem to be advancing faster because Ms. Quality makes better use of her time with the students than Mr. Quantity. Her focus on student achievement serves her better than Mr. Quantity's scattered approach. Granted, there are variables like quality of students, but, all things being equal, the teacher who seeks to make the most of their time with their students seems to get better results.

There is certainly a quantity of time we must spend at any job to avoid dismissal or failure. Even as a self-employed person, I must put in a certain number of hours each week to insure keeping my job. Beyond that, however, what we attempt to accomplish while at work (quality) is what sometimes brings the raises, bonuses, or career satisfaction.

In my current role as a speaker, I work with various private and government institutions. When I meet personally with their planning committees or directors, it is quickly apparent who believes in quality versus quantity time. Some members of the committee will simply serve as dead weight or devil's advocates to new ideas and have no desire to see a project reach its potential... they are simply biding their time. Others, however, are ready to make things happen, to stretch beyond mediocrity to create a program that has a high standard of excellence. The dead weight will complain of too many responsibilities but after the meeting spend excessive time on the phone, shuffle papers, and find other things to do. They may even work on Saturday or during the evening, but if you examine their activities during the day, you might be surprised to see their lack of productivity.

Again, a disclaimer. Some jobs require incredible time commitments and work on weekends. While writing this book, it was necessary for me to get up each morning at 5:00 AM until it was completed to be able to get the book finished while still meeting other professional and personal obligations. When the ox is in the ditch, we have to get it out (translated: There are times when one must do things that we would like to put off until later). My fear, however, is that many people simply trudge off to work, filling their quantity requirements, and then return home. They will openly express their discontent with their job and/or job problems but are not willing to put in the quality time to improve their situation.

During my first years in public speaking, my promotional packet consisted of a cassette tape of program excerpts, reference letters, brochures, and program outlines. The industry standard, however, requires a demo videotape since people want to see what they are planning to use. As much as I wanted to resist the increased cost and production of a videotape, I knew that no matter how many hours I worked (quantity), the absence of a videotape would adversely affect my chances for success.

When people tell you about their unhappiness in a job or career, they no doubt have valid reasons for their discontent. To determine if they are willing to improve their situation, ask them what they have done or are doing to make things more bearable. If they mention nothing more than showing up or verbally complaining, then they shouldn't expect things to miraculously turn around any time soon. You may even want to do them a favor and tell them that.

Determining the Winner

Finding the balance between quality and quantity time is extremely person specific. In relationships, the best determinant may be, "Do I spend enough time with this person (quantity) to be able to know their needs and make them happy (quality)." In our careers the question becomes, "While fulfilling the minimum time requirements for my job (quantity), am I actively engaged in those activities that will insure my success and that of the company (quality)?" Merely attempting to concentrate on one or the other brings us back to the chocolate chip cookies and cheesecake. I don't know about you, but I want my cake and cookies, too. The right balance may offer us the sweet satisfaction we so desperately seek in life.

R

Resolving Conflict

How many times does it happen? We start trying to discuss a problem and soon find ourselves yelling at each other about things that have nothing to do with the original problem. We then go our separate ways, sometimes saying extremely unkind things about the other person or people involved in our conflict. Reconciliation comes only when the thorn in the relationship has become so severe that it paralyzes us professionally or personally.

Sound familiar? It does to me. But then again I am a male. Males tend to like conflict because it gives them a chance to be conquerors...review the chapter on working together. It is my experience that the reason for the conflict falls into one of three areas:

Postponed problems...Theirs and Yours

In college, my friends and I loved to play a game called Jenga. In that game you have a stack of similarly sized blocks of wood. The object is to remove a block from the bottom and then place it on top of the stack without the stack falling. That's how many relationships function as well. We all have our problems or hang-ups that annoy others, but things go pretty well as long as there are no external pressures acting on the relationship. Apply pressure to the relationship, however (i.e. unclear expectations, broken trust, financial problems), and things get a little shaky. Soon more pressures act on the relationship before the instability is corrected, and our foundation becomes even more shaky. Finally, one seemingly insignificant shift takes place in the relationship, and CRASH! it all falls apart. By postponing action on previous problems, we set ourselves up for a game that is not fun to play.

Prepared to Pounce
Ever watch a cat stalking a bird or other prey? Whether it's an alley cat or a tiger, the process is usually the same. They remain perfectly motionless, watching their potential meal move around until just the right moment and...whoosh! They dart in at just the right moment to capture the unsuspecting object. Trying to talk with other people can sometimes be a similar situation, especially if you are trying to discuss something that will return stability to the relationship. In short, they hear what they want instead of listening to the entire conservation to get a grasp of the big picture.

Several years ago my future wife and I served as counselors for a foundation that conducted youth leadership conferences in a number of states in the Southeast. The workshop we led was entitled "Moral Courage." The gist of the workshop was that we discussed the possible effects of inappropriate music, TV shows, movies, and books. The goal was simply to get the participants thinking about how we can all become desensitized to negative messages and allow more negative ones to infiltrate our lives. The mode of operation in the workshop was that we would all read a section together silently and then discuss it. Remember, the goal was discussion.

The students, on the other hand, saw it differently. They saw the workshop as an attack on their interests and would wait until something they read did not fit their way of thinking. At that point you could see the claws extend and the glare develop in their eyes. The workshop had multiple sessions, and each progressing session seemed to get quieter as many of the students got into position to attack what they read that they did not agree with rather than look at the concepts being presented. They heard nothing else because they were waiting for just the right moment to verbally "jump" on our comments and "kill" any hope of a productive discussion.

No doubt you too have had similar expenses. The person you are attempting to communicate with normally stares at you intently, sometimes nodding their head in agreement. Their goal is to get you to hurry up and finish your stuff so they can take off on their point. Your input is practically useless because they are only interested in letting you know where you were wrong in your thoughts.

Past Performance

We all hold grudges against other people. Well, I'm sure *you* don't, but for those of us who do, they often lead to inflated conflicts. As we listen to others explain their plight, we turn off to those things we have heard before, skeptical of their sincerity. Often we do not hide our doubt very well. The other person senses that, and begins to question the possibility of a resolution.

Solutions to these problems

Postponed Problems: Be a bottle of *Drano* and not a plunger. Let's review some plumbing basics. When you have a clog in a sink, you have two options. One is to insert a plunger into the drain and, with a certain amount of physical force, push the clog out of the drain line. The only problem with this approach is that you normally have to remove all the items in the sink, bail out the water, and later clean up the mess. That's just the way most of us approach conflict. We wait until it builds up to a bursting point and then force an answer, usually causing residual problems. Now to option two. When you observe that your sink is draining more slowly than usual, add the recommended amount of *Drano*. The clog remover will find the source of the problem without force and return the drain to normal operation. In other words, when you first notice signs of problems within a relationship, find the source by asking the right questions (to be discussed later) and having a genuine desire to restore the relationship.

Prepared to Pounce: This one is not so easily solved. As a teacher, my wife used a system with her students that worked pretty well. When talking with a student about a confrontational issue, she would have the student repeat back the key thoughts she had presented. Many times when someone has to recall information, they are required to look at the big picture and not just repeat the point of conflict. For me it helps to remind myself (and the other person) of the desired results of our conversation and/or relationship (completed project, improved working environment, more intimate relationship).

Past Performance: As a teacher I had several students who were chronic behavior problems. They did not carry guns or attack people in class, but they were constant distractions. During my first year of teaching, when I knew everything, I would conference with them and tell them how many times that had misbehaved or disrupted class. It became a standing joke with them as they would ask, "Okay, Mr. Loflin, how many does that make for the year?" I eventually learned that a better way to approach them was simply to state the required operation of class (no disruptive behavior or failure to follow instructions) and explain that they were not meeting it. I would even go so far as to ask them, "Why did I keep you after class?" Their response was normally honest and got to the point much quicker than my review of past behaviors. If you must bring up past behaviors, make sure you address how you genuinely want to improve the situation.

Putting the puzzle together vs. preparing to do battle

We have already discussed the reasons why conflicts arise in our lives. Now the question becomes, "How do I resolve it without destroying the relationship?" The first step is to crystallize your thoughts so that there will be at least one level-headed person in the conversation.

1) Ride the Seesaw, Forget the Swing.

As you begin looking at solving a conflict with someone, remember to focus on solving the problem to increase the effectiveness of your relationship, association, and/or individual roles. The childhood playground provides an excellent example for us.

Let's suppose the objective for you and your friend is to have fun. The playground has one swing, some monkey bars, and a seesaw. You begin by playing on the monkey bars with each of you doing your own thing. You are meeting your objective individually, not dependent on the other for your fun. In a perfect (or lonely, depending on your viewpoint) world, it would be great if we were not dependent on each other for our happiness and productivity. Eventually, however, we do need each other, and problems arise.

Having tired of playing on the monkey bars, you both move to the swing. A problem arises...how will you both meet your objective when there is only one swing? They share the swing with one pushing the other, having a wonderful time. Soon, however, problems arise. One got to ride the swing longer than the other or one pushes too hard or one is bored. I realize the importance of sharing and how they should take turns, but there must be a way where you can both achieve your objective at the same time. Transfer the swing mentality to a conflict. If our idea of solving the conflict is simply to get the other person to feel bad or admit wrongdoing (get off the swing) so you can feel better (get on the swing), you have not solved the problem. You have actually added to its complexity as you have introduced new issues into the conflict that have nothing to do with the original problem.

Finally, one of you spots the seesaw. You rush to it and get on simultaneously. You both laugh with glee as you go up and down, both meeting your original objective of having fun. By focusing on your objective (to have fun), you can use both person's insights and opinions (weight) to make something positive happen (both can have fun on the seesaw). Granted not all situations will allow for everyone to totally meet their objective, but if we work from the reference point of meeting them, the playground of life will be much more fun for everyone.

2) Seek the why before you say "I".

Two of my favorite things to say in an argument are, "I want to know why you did that!" or "I have had about all I can take!" Even if I don't say it, that is often an underlying thought when I approach a conflict. My idea is that if they understand how frustrated or disappointed I am, they will come over to my way of thinking and see that they are wrong. Brilliant, huh? That approach is flawless *if* the other person or people have no ideas, thoughts or opinions of their own.

Some time ago I was part of a planning group for a community youth rally. Six to eight people gathered and began to make plans for the activity. Early in the meeting one person suggested that we block off main street in this little community. Another person immediately jumped on the idea and announced that, "It can't be done because of state highway guidelines." Another person became involved and suggested that we contact a regional representative to get approval. Another suggested that we send a contingency of key people to talk with the highway commission to get approval. Another member of the committee then discussed the problems related to fire and rescue access. After about ten minutes of round about discussion, one person in the group asked, "Why do you want to close off the street?" The original person's reply was simple: "I just want to make sure we have enough room for everyone." Once that was said, the demeanor of the entire group changed. People started suggesting alternative locations if the streets could not be closed. In less than five minutes the location had been determined.

It was not until someone asked "Why" that the group once again became productive. Once we sincerely begin to attempt to understand the background, opinions, and frustrations of the other person, we make tremendous strides toward positive solutions. We are more free to share our thoughts from our point of view and have a blueprint on which to build an acceptable solution.

3) Think MacGyver and not the Road Runner and the Coyote.

While growing up, I loved to watch Warner Brothers cartoons. One of my favorites was the *Road Runner and the Coyote.* Being a short, overweight little boy, I guess I loved the idea of being so swift. Now let's review the story line. Wiley Coyote's (Wiley happens to be my first name) goal was always to capture the road runner and have him for a meal. Not being as fast at the road runner, however, the coyote had to resort to numerous gadgets or schemes to capture the road runner. They normally involved dropping something on the road runner or igniting some type of explosive rocket device to try to match his incredible speed.

The coyote failed miserably time after time. Why? Because he used the same types of solutions over and over. At five years of age I found myself often screaming at the coyote, "It won't work...you tried that last week!"

When people work through conflict, they frequently reflect the same thought process as the coyote. They try the same tired solutions to a problem, already knowing the outcome will not provide the desired results. What happens? Just like the coyote, they suffer a fall that inflicts emotional and sometimes physical pain not only on themselves but also those they are attempting to reconcile with.

The way we should think is like MacGyver. *MacGyver* was a TV show about an undercover FBI agent who was constantly rescuing hostages, retrieving stolen goods, or, in general, just insuring that humanity was safe from the evils of the world (the story line of a thousand shows). The difference with MacGyver, however, was that he was often caught by the bad guys or stuck in a life-threatening situation. Facing those situations, he would look around his area, evaluating every miniscule item in the room and how it could be used individually or as part of an assembly to get him out of his situation. In one episode, he was trapped in a bank vault and escaped using only a match, bubble gum, and a paper clip.

The MacGyver approach to resolving conflicts offers a multitude of solutions compared to the coyote thought process. By stopping to think about creative solutions to solving our conflict, we begin to use the "items" (goals of individuals, groups, relationships) around us to piece together a solution that will get us out of our situation. The key is that we have to be creative and not just order the latest item from Acme (the company that the coyote always got his stuff).

Putting It All Together

I know what you are saying by now: "Jones, I'm growing weary of all this stuff about thought processes and ways to look at *resolving* the conflict. I want to know how to actually solve it." I agree. However, the key to resolving many conflicts is the preparation before the actual verbal discussion (not confrontation). Recall the process for going on a family vacation or trip of a few days in length. Perhaps you are wealthy enough to just jump in the car and go, planning to buy things as you need them. More likely, however, you will take a few moments to plan what items to pack and then actually put them in some type of carrying device. By planning your approach and mindset to removing the wedge in the relationship before actually engaging in the conversation, you may find that you have the items necessary to make it a much more pleasant and profitable experience.

The Actual Encounter

Having gotten yourself in order, approach the other person with this process:

Step 1) Say *"I have a problem"* or *"I need your help."* Now don't jump on my case just yet. You're thinking, "But the problem is not with me, it's with them." Okay, do it your way. Start your conversation by using one of these classic lines:

"We need to talk."

"I need to talk to you."

"You have a problem, and we need to talk about it."

"Can I talk with you about something that's been bothering me?"

Watch, then, as the hair rises on the back of their neck like a cat being confronted by a dog. Watch as the walls of defensiveness go up, and they respond with some phrase that reminds you that they are ready to do battle if necessary.

By saying "I have a problem" instead, we are inviting that person to listen and to help with the solution. It creates an atmosphere of support instead of one of animosity. By using "I need your help" you are already letting them know that their support and assistance will improve your well being. Even in today's "me" society, most people still have a heart of compassion for those in need.

The idea of saying "I have a problem" would have helped tremendously in a situation I observed at a high school assembly. Following my program to the students in grades 9-12, the principal dismissed everyone except the junior class. I wondered why they were being kept in the gym and asked several students if they knew. They speculated it was something about class officers, class rings, or some other facet of school life. Once the other students had left the gym, the principal said, "Officer Johnson needs to talk with you about something." The atmosphere in the gym changed almost immediately. The expressions on their faces turned sour, and there was a marked shuffling of feet and bodies. If that was not bad enough, the principal offered the police officer the microphone, but he declined, saying, "I don't need that, I'll just talk loud." He then proceeded to say, "Some of you are in trouble." You can guess the rest. The officer made a blanket accusation of all the students about graffiti on local bridges, etc., and threatened not to allow future homecoming parades because of "their" misbehavior. I doubt most students ever heard a word he said after the first few moments. They were too busy thinking about all the things they disliked about him. I asked the principal later if this group had been a problem class, and he said, "No, we just want to remind them of what can happen if they do not follow the rules." My thought... Okay, you assisted in damaging the relationship between the police officer and the students and probably created a level of distrust toward your own administration. One problem solved, two others created.

Having been a school teacher, I realize the need to be firm and that sometimes the final way to deal with a student is to call attention to their behavior, tell them the consequences, and then secure their commitment to improve in the future. However, how can we expect to improve the cooperation skills of our young people (a quality grossly lacking in both youth and adults) if we do not attempt to use that as a first option in resolving problems?

I stood back as I was listening to the police officer and imagined a much different approach. The principal had handed the microphone to the police officer, who would have said in a normal tone of voice, "I have a problem." An opportunity for humor arises (a great tension remover) as the officer says, "Many of you would say that I have a lot of problems, but today I want to talk about just one." From there he would proceed to step 2 with a much more cooperative audience.

Step 2) Give a non threatening description of the problem from your viewpoint.

Another benchmark mistake at this point is to attempt to establish guilt or blame. Phrases like:

"You need to stop..."   *"You should start..."*
"The problem is that you keep..."

serve only to raise the walls of defensiveness in the other person. One usual mental reaction of the other person is to begin recalling your imperfections and shortcomings as ammunition for upcoming battles in this conversation.

A more effective alternative is to give a description of the problem from your viewpoint. Talk about what you have observed or noticed. You now come across as a person who genuinely wants to discuss a problem instead of as a dictator who is handing down his/her ruling on another person.

Let's look at an example. As an employer you have an employee who is constantly late for meetings. The old approach is to go to the employee and say, "You need to be on time for meetings" and then leave the employee to their work. Don't be surprised if at the next meeting your employee makes a cutting remark if the meeting does not start on time. Your dictatorial statement may have made you feel good about your superiority, but you may have done considerable harm to the relationship. In these days of reduced employee loyalty, the working environment created by positive or negative relationships goes a long way toward retaining those employees who can make your organization a success.

Using our new found information, we approach the employee and say, "Jones, I have noticed than when we have our weekly meetings, you are sometimes 10 or 15 minutes late." Let's evaluate your statement. You have not told them their actions are wrong. They may infer that you are telling them they are wrong, but that is much different from you confronting them with it. In fact, they may actually begin to realize the detrimental effects of their behavior on their own, a huge step on the road to self-improvement. Again, our desire in this step is to get the problem on the table, not to make a case about how right you are or how wrong they are.

Step 3) Tell how the situation makes you feel.

By now you are literally screaming, "When do I get to tell them they are wrong, and I am right!" Be patient, my friend. Remember our previous section on your thought processes when dealing with conflict. Our objective is to improve the effectiveness of the relationship. At this point in the conversation, it is time to share your feelings about the situation. In relationships between logical people (we'll assume the other person *is* logical), there is a tendency to be more willing to change negative behaviors if the person sees that it is having a specific negative effect on someone. Simply let them know you are frustrated, disappointed, angered, or even confused when the situation occurs. Your goal is to let them see how you feel, not to make them feel guilt.

Returning to our chronically late employee, we say, "Jones, I am uncomfortable with this situation because I can not allow my other employees to be late for the meeting" or "Jones, I am confused by this situation because we have our meetings at the same time every week." They are most likely feeling guilt at this point. Not so much guilt about their being late for meetings but about disappointing someone in their circle of relationships.

Step 4) Ask about the long term effects to your relationship.
The question, "If this behavior continues, will it make our relationship better or worse?" makes a quantum leap in the direction of setting up solutions to the problem. The other person now sees that you are not attacking them about a single problem but are concerned about the future welfare of the relationship. Their most likely response to the question will be "worse," which brings us to step 5.

Step 5) Ask, "Do you want our relationship to get better or worse?"
A response of "better" gives you a more open door through which to discuss the problem and its sources in hopes of a creative solution. Of course, if they fail to respond "better" or give no response, the problem may go much deeper than being late for a weekly meeting. If that is the case, then the underlying causes can be more easily discussed because at least one of you has expressed an interest in improving the relationship. It is not a right vs. wrong argument.

Summing It Up
If your head is spinning after reading this chapter, don't feel bad. There are literally hundreds of methods to use in resolving conflicts with other people. Check out the self-help section at any bookstore and many of the books will focus on creating a more effective

relationship with other people. While all this information exists, the problem is still a complex one since it involves people's emotions, which are subject to quickly change.

   To attempt to get through the conflict alive and maintain the integrity of all parties, make a point to separate the person from the problem. Your goal should always be to solve the problem and in the process, improve your relationship with the other person. If you choose to make it a "win-lose" situation, remember that one day you might be on the losing end of the argument. (it happens to the best of us) I don't know about you, but I would rather have people looking out for my best interests instead of looking for ways to harm me emotionally, mentally or even physically. Lastly, realize that you cannot control them nor can you make them react a certain way. Like you, they have their own "hot buttons" and imperfections. You can only control your own thoughts, words and actions and hope that your comments are taken sincerely by the other person. Who knows, they may even choose to model your example. Remember the quotation, "Imitation is the most sincere form of flattery."

S

Savage

Okay, so maybe I am stretching just a wee bit with this one. As you have probably read from the table of contents, this chapter will deal with meal and restaurant etiquette. Sure, it would probably fit better into the image section, but then I would not have had an interesting chapter for the letter "S." On a serious note, though, I believe our professionalism at meal time reflects greatly upon who we are in other situations.

Several years ago a CEO became well known for his skill in choosing the best people for positions within his company. His secret was extreme but hints at the significance of dining habits. For interviews for upper level management positions, the CEO would include a meal at a local restaurant. After they received their food, he would watch the potential employee. If he salted his food before tasting it, he was denied the position with the company. The CEO's rationale was that if they would make a decision (salting their food) before getting all the information first (tasting the food), they would not function well with the difficult decisions to made in corporate America. Extreme, yes, but all of us can recall times when a dining experience with someone highlighted a sloppy or unpleasant nature.

In my training conferences for youth and adults, I have increasingly been asked to include a session on meal and restaurant etiquette. The reasons are obvious. Youth officers, especially on a state and national level, are frequently invited to represent the organization at awards programs or other activities. Those meetings almost always include a meal function. To present anything less than a professional image at those functions gives a lackluster impression of the organization one is representing. From an adult's perspective, good manners are an excellent addition to the image tool box, whether one serves as an officer or is interviewing for a job. In these situations I normally prepare a formal table setting and discuss the meal, followed by tips on exhibiting professionalism in restaurant settings.

Another disclaimer: Martha Stewart I am not. In fact, Lisa gets a big belly laugh each time she hears that I will be teaching dining etiquette. I have never claimed to be an expert on much of anything. My approach to etiquette is more of "common sense" etiquette. I call a case knife a butter knife and could not actually tell you which way to properly dip a soup spoon into the bowl. Guess what? Ninety percent of the population probably does not know either. I do review proper dining etiquette before attending a formal gathering but do not focus on the minute details of the correct way to wash your fingers in a finger bowl before attending an outdoor barbecue. In matters of etiquette I believe that we should teach broad concepts that will cover a wide range of circumstances.

My thoughts on etiquette may derive from a psychologically damaging experience while in middle school. In a class called Occupational Exploration, we had the opportunity to learn about careers in areas ranging from horticulture to industry to business. One of our instructors was a lady who had a great desire to instill in us uncultured louts the value of good manners, from saying "Yes Ma'am" to opening the door for a lady. She also wanted us to look professional even while we ate. Each nine weeks (class rotation) she would have a lunch at school in which each student would supply their own steak and she would provide the trimmings. While it seemed like a great experience, there was a problem. She believed that left-handed people should learn to cut steak as a right-handed person. She would even stand behind us while we were sitting and imitate the correct movements by putting her arms around us. I'd love to see her try it today!

I'm left-handed and have experienced all the challenges faced by lefties in this world. I saw no reason to change my cutting hand just because it might appear "less professional" to my teacher. That one experience ingrained within me a distaste for getting wrapped up in every small detail of formal etiquette. Couple that with my desire to make everything practical, and it is painfully obvious that I will never dine with royalty.

Since recreating the dining environment would be clumsy on paper, allow me to utilize one of my favorite techniques in sharing some tips about meal etiquette: A Top Ten List. One common thread binding all these tips together is the need to adapt to your environment. Your dining habits with friends or family will be much different than those with strangers or potential business partners. The key is knowing what is acceptable behavior.

Top Ten Things To Remember In Matters of Dining Etiquette

10) Be the host(ess) with the most(est). To establish an air of professionalism about yourself, take the lead at your table if no one has been appointed in an official capacity. If others appear uncomfortable or unsure about what to do, make them feel at ease. Be the first to welcome people to the table and keep others involved in the table talk. You will be remembered much longer for being a great conversationalist than for knowing the proper way to eat your bread.

9) Do not serve whine with every meal. As Abraham Lincoln once said, "It is better to be quiet and thought a fool, than to open your mouth and prove it." If you are unsure about the proper etiquette at a meal function, watch those around you. Never announce to the group that you are ignorant of such things.

While attending meal functions in my capacity as a speaker, I will sometimes sit with a group in the audience. Within a few minutes someone at the table will make a joke about not knowing etiquette or which tea glass is theirs. Why don't they just wave a banner that says, "I am insecure right now, and my escape is to joke about it." Be discreet at meal time. Calling attention to your ignorance (or defiance) of how to eat like a professional only serves to create a belief in those around you that you are less than confident about yourself.

Another item that irks me is people who complain about the food at the table. Someone at the table may have helped sponsor the meal. To gripe about its quality may cause hard feelings that result in problems later. Also, avoid getting caught up in a riot. At a dinner table someone may begin complaining about the food and several members of the group join the mob that wants to verbally lynch the server or chef. Refrain from joining their unhappy alliance at all costs. If asked your opinion of the food, be polite and brief. Say nothing more.

8) When you're right, you're right. Pass dishes of food to the right. You should be the last to receive it. It is the same for salt and pepper or containers of sugar, butter, etc. When passing the salt and pepper, both should be passed even if one is requested. Your beverage cups or glasses will begin near the top of your plate and continue down the right side. As for silverware, you begin with the outermost utensils. The salad fork will be on the outside followed by the dinner fork. The dessert fork or spoon will typically be placed at the top of your dinner plate if not brought with the dessert. People seem to get especially confused at round tables where the dinnerware is packed together to accommodate a large number of people. When in doubt, look at the head table. The end seats will provide clues as to the location of your utensils, salad and bread plates, and beverage glasses.

7) Avoid the hog-at-the-trough syndrome. In extremely large banquets you will see salads already in place before the function begins. In those cases it is appropriate to begin eating. In other cases, however, one should wait until all the individuals at your table have been served before eating. Pacing your meal is also important. Watch those around you. Are you the first one to complete the meal? If so, you may be eating too fast. Perhaps they are attempting to take the dishes away while you are still enjoying your salad. You may want to pick up the pace just a bit. Eating as though you are the only one at the table is a major sign of a lack of courtesy to others.

Now some of my pet peeves in this area. Avoid carving meat on your plate into twenty pieces at one time. Most guides say to cut no more than two bites at a time. Doing so helps slow your pace during the meal. Yes, I know it is wasted movement to keep putting the knife down time after time, but remember that this meal is a social experience as much as it is a way to provide nourishment. Giving the appearance that you have not eaten in days is poor form to say the least. Also, avoid snorting or squealing like a pig. What I am referring to is smelling your food for approval (snorting) or frequently commenting on the quality of the meal (squealing). Either gives the appearance that you do not get out much. If you are unsure of what an item on your plate is, discreetly ask the waiter/waitress what the item is or ask the person next to you. Do not announce to the entire group that you have never seen Chicken Cordon Bleu.

Lastly, avoid making a butter sandwich. A hot roll with melted butter is next to euphoria for me but is inappropriate in formal situations. Bread should be torn in halves or quarters and only the portion being eaten should be buttered.

6) Perform the great napkin disappearing act. Once seated, the napkin goes in the lap. There is dissension in the ranks on what to do if you must leave the table for a moment. Some books say to neatly fold it and place it to the left of your plate. Others say to leave it in your seat. My procedure is to leave it in the seat. Why? Because I am a messy eater. Try as I may, I regularly have to wipe sauce from my mouth or clean up a small spill around my plate. My napkin speaks volumes about my meal, so the last thing I want is for someone to see it while I'm eating. Leaving it in the chair preserves my reputation. Once the meal function is over (not the meal), the napkin should be lightly folded (not wadded) and placed to the left of the plate. Covering your plate or dessert dish like you are hiding something is not appropriate.

5) Do not dump your trash in my back yard. With the salad you need crackers. To sweeten the tea (I am from the South) you need packs of sweetener or sugar. Butter wrappers may also be in your area as well as coffee creamer containers. By the end of the meal you have a multi-colored pile of trash screaming, "Look at this guy, what a messy person!" As you open packs, place them under the lip of your bread dish or dinner plate. Get them out of plain view. When servers arrive to collect your salad plate or dinner dish, you can discreetly place them on the plate or under another dish. Keeping your dining space neat and orderly signals an attention to detail.

4) Wands are for waving, utensils are for eating. We have all been guilty of this violation at one time or another. In heated debate or lively discussion, we want to make an impassioned point about something. Not having time to put down our fork, we point it at someone or wave it in the air while talking. Each time I see this happen, it reminds me of a mother who is about to levy a verbal lashing on a child and is pointing "the finger" at them. Refrain from waving silverware while talking or getting someone's attention. A good rule of thumb is to remember that when silverware is in hand, do not talk. Again, the meal is a social experience. Gluing the utensils to your hand so you can wolf down your food is not the way to win the respect of others.

3) Concrete needs mixing, cake batter needs mixing, but most foods do not. Being from the South, I have a tendency to mix foods in my plate. That pork chop would taste so much better if I slid it into the mashed potatoes before placing it in my mouth. The rule of thumb, however, is that if the foods are served separately on your plate, they should be eaten separately. If you have baked chicken served on rice or something similar, they can be mixed.

This brings me to another pet peeve when eating…the use of sauces. I am a heavy ketchup user when I eat French fries and enjoy occasional steak sauce with red meat. However, I do not marinate my French fries before eating, nor do I see just how much sauce I can get on my steak before it runs into the baked potato or rice pilaf. Sauces are meant to be placed on one section of the plate and foods dipped into them. Don't try to hoard the sauce either. If you run out, there will be more. If not, what have you lost? I see some young people who must believe the one with the most ketchup on their plate at the end of the meal gets the prize. When you have finished eating, your plate should be as neat as possible. As I say that, I cringe because it brings up another point.

Most hotels and catering facilities have excellent dishwashing equipment. You have little need to assist them in cleaning the plates by rubbing your bread over it. Yes, that gravy was to die for, but you are not an incarcerated criminal enjoying his last meal. If you really must have more, go to the restaurant in the hotel or conference center. Usually they serve similar fare there and you can have all your heart desires of the heavenly stuff.

2) Blowing your nose is not a mating call. I have a stomach of steel. I am not talking about my superb muscle condition in that area, however. I am referring to my ability to eat while there are things going on around me that could encourage me to stop. However, other people are not always as relaxed in their eating routine. Blowing your nose, cleaning your fingernails, or performing any other bodily activity at meal time should be confined to the restroom or hallway. You will have the occasional sneeze or cough that cannot be controlled, but in most cases, the other behaviors come as we get bored or are nervous in a meeting. One unconscious moment, and you are biting your finger to remove that last hang nail. I have an occasional scalp problem and must be careful not to scratch my head during those periods. Consistently scratching my head sends negative signals to others at my table. The flakes on my shoulder also add to their perception of me as an untidy individual.

1) Conversation should encourage bonding, not indigestion. The old saying is "Never discuss politics or religion." No doubt those are two prime subjects of debate, but I believe others can sour a conversation just as quickly. One is a discussion of sexual orientation. My friends are all gasping as they read this part. No, I have no need to come out of the closet with anything as one TV character recently did, but I do believe that we have to be aware of the fact that those around us may not have the same beliefs we do. You may not be in the presence of someone with those tendencies, but the person at your table may know someone who does fit the description. Bashing a group or offering your wholesale opinion on them will only serve to drive a wedge between you and that other person that will not easily be removed. You can quickly be viewed as narrow-minded, especially if those around you don't know much about you. If asked your opinion, honestly share it but maintain your tactfulness and professionalism while doing so.

Another area of sure discourse is in family relationships. In my workshops I frequently ask, "Are you married?" when I work with an adult volunteer in front of the group. I usually need their spouse's name to make it personal. Indeed, asking the question is most likely harmless, but our society has changed so much that we cannot take anything for granted. Asking about someone's marital status may conjure up memories of a relationship gone bad or perhaps even one quickly deteriorating. It is too late to save the conversation when the person is too noticeably tense or nervous to give an answer. You spend the rest of the meal attempting to restore the person's trust in you and make them feel comfortable again. It rarely happens.

Inquiring about children can be dangerous as well. We have a neighbor whose marriage failed due in part to their inability to have children. Yes, I believe the husband was extremely pigheaded, but that I cannot change. We like to spend time with this lady because she is witty, caring, and a joy to be around. However, when our young daughter is along, we can sense the uneasiness when we discuss Alex or focus the conversation on her. Infertility is a common problem in today's world, and some couples are very private about such things. Add to that the insecurity of parents with wayward children, and we have a recipe for disaster when pressing for personal information.

Does this mean we should not ask at all? Of course not. Listen (see jabber chapter) for key words that will allow you to discern what would be acceptable or unacceptable to talk about. In talking with me, you will quickly learn that family matters are pretty much fair game. Others may not be so inclined. Instead, focus on their professional responsibilities and interests. Be complimentary of whatever job they have, and make it a point to really get to know the person in that area. A focused, personal approach to conversation will help you remember that person later and make the other person feel a renewed sense of self-confidence because you took the time to get to know them.

If table talk is not your forte, quickly review the headlines in the newspaper. To be up to speed on local issues, I frequently stop by the newspaper boxes and jot down the headlines and other lead stories on the front page. People are terribly impressed when you know what is going on in their neck of the woods. If the meeting includes people from all across the United States, get a *USA Today*. In addition to scanning the headlines, glance at the states page, which contains the major stories for each state. Our minds are wonderful computers, and even if you quickly read through the notes, you will be amazed how much you actually retain when someone mentions their home state.

A few thoughts about restaurant etiquette

Tipping is mandatory. There is no other sign of poor judgement or a lack of professional courtesy more noticeable than inappropriate tipping. A minimum of 15% if reasonable service has been received. Don't be petty about reasonable service, either. To expect them to cater to your every whim (especially if you are a whiner) is not simply reasonable, but is preferential and should be tipped accordingly. Set up your standards for reasonable service before going to a restaurant. A key factor for me is the filling of my beverage glass. I drink a lot of water or tea at meal-time and want to the same courtesy when I'm in a restaurant. Asking twice for a refill is not reasonable to me. Another signal of good service to me is whether the waiter or waitress really asks about the taste of the food or quality of our dining experience. I say "really" because we have all had the paper-delivery waiter who threw the question out on their way to the kitchen or to assist another customer. Again, I do not expect them to sit down and allow me to evaluate each vegetable or the lighting in the room. Coming to a complete stop and actually facing me is not asking too much. If they are attentive to my needs by stopping to genuinely ask, they usually can take care of problems like slow food service or improperly cooked entrees.

Lack of change or the appropriate correct change is no excuse for not tipping either. What if your employer told you that since they did not want to transfer funds from an existing account, they rounded off your paycheck to the nearest five dollars? You would not be a happy camper. Tips can be placed on credit cards, or you can step to the cashier while on a trip to the restroom and get what you need. If figuring the tip is difficult for you, simply take the total amount of the bill and move the decimal one place to the left. That is ten percent.

Double that amount and you have twenty percent. If you take ten percent of the total bill and add half of that to the ten percent, that is fifteen percent. Think I am being too elementary with this math lesson? You obviously have not eaten with some of the people I have. Having completed this math exercise, they now have no excuse except for being a cheapskate.

Be the Lone Ranger. For the generations who have no knowledge of the Lone Ranger, a brief aside. The TV show by the same name was set in the Old West. When people were in danger from thieves or any potentially threatening situation, a masked man (with a Native American assistant) would arrive just in the nick of time to save the day. No one ever knew his identity, but they were grateful for his assistance.

Problems will arise when dining as a group in a restaurant. Someone will not get what they ordered or have a water glass that is empty of anything but ice. The table may lack a salt shaker or a setting of silverware. Most people are impatient, and if the deficiency is not readily resolved, one person's negative vibes can infuse the rest of the group. The disgruntled person with the empty tea glass can cause someone who is otherwise perfectly satisfied to complain about the condition of their meal.

As a teacher I took many students on field trips. My worst nightmare when on these trips was if something was not perfect with a meal I had planned or the location chosen by the group. If something was amiss, the students would not only complain while at the restaurant but would harbor ill feelings for years to come. We adults are much the same. Have a good dining experience and little is made of it. Have a bad one, and we bring it up time and time again.

When someone is less than content and the waiter or waitress does not show a quick willingness to resolve the crisis, excuse yourself from the table. On your way to the restroom or to make a phony phone call, find the waiter or waitress and relate to them the need to take care of the problem. Taking the time to find the waiter usually signals that they need to give your request serious consideration. If they seem indifferent, find the host or manager and politely recruit their assistance. Return to the table and tell no one of your adventure but give yourself a private pat on the back for helping others have a more pleasurable dining experience. It may actually make yours more enjoyable, too.

Be discreet. If you are experiencing a problem with your meal in a restaurant, handle it as discreetly as possible. Ask the waiter/waitress for the necessary assistance, and expect it to be handled. Stewing over the issue just sends your negative germs to others at your table. If a problem continues, seek the manager, not by yelling so loud that half the restaurant can hear you, but by privately speaking to him or her. Don't ruin someone else's meal because yours is less than expected. Reflect it in the tip or comment card and/or speak with the manager. If you really want results, write a letter and indicate that a copy is being sent to a local agency like the Chamber of Commerce or Better Business Bureau. Ask me about the power of that avenue sometime. The results you will get are incredible.

Clearing the Table

Leslie Matthews, a consultant with the NC Department of Public Instruction, gave me a thought that I think best sums up an effective approach to meal and restaurant etiquette. It is called the Three C's. If a situation arises in etiquette and you are unsure how to respond, ask:

Is it Courteous?   *Is it Convenient?*
Does it show Common sense?

After reading this chapter you may feel lacking in the formal social graces. If so, any number of books or manuals on the subject are available from the library or book store. My personal favorite is *How Rude*, by Dr. Alex J. Packer. The thoughts in this chapter were offered to give you a mode of operation to use in almost any situation ranging from eating pizza from a box to a seven-course meal. Following these steps will not insure your place in the Etiquette Hall of Fame but will allow you to dine with a degree of comfort and help hide the savage that lives within each of us.

T

Time Management

Just as the words "I love you" make up the most overused phrase in our relationships, the words "I do not have time" make up the most abused phrase in response to commitments. In almost every conversation with a friend, the phrase is communicated either directly or by implication. It is used for everything from explaining why we did not return a phone call to rationalizing our failure to accomplish a seemingly major goal in our lives.

The effective management of time is one of my burning passions in life. You will remember that I shared some people's misconceptions about me in the optical illusions chapter. The pre-conceived notion that I am a preacher most often arises when I am completing a time-management seminar. People will say, "I have been to many time-management seminars, but yours was by far the most emotional and intense workshop about what I have always considered a dry topic." I am humbled by such comments and must admit that I may get a bit too carried away at times. My passion arises, however, because if there is one thing all of us (and I do mean *all*) can do to insure a better future, it is to make the most of our time resources. I have yet to meet someone who cannot find any activities or habits to change in order to spend more time with more important things. Unless, of course, you are the parents of the septuplets born in Iowa in November, 1997. They probably have little leeway in adjusting their schedule.

Desires vs. Demands

Another source of my passion when sharing thoughts on time management is that many seminars lack a focus on the desire. In other words, what do you *desire* to do with your time resources or time not spent on completing a required task? Instead, most seminars look at the demand side. The demand side says, "How can I spend less time on this task to meet my demands in other areas of my life?" It includes tips, tricks, and a host of other strategies to be a top-notch employee or maximize productivity. While all those things are necessary, without desire the workshop comes up short. It does not invite the participant to say, "Okay, now that I am spending less time on this activity or series of activities, it will allow me to…" I may know the way to the bank, but unless I have a reason to go there (withdraw money), I am not likely to drive by just to make sure it still exists. By the same token, I may want to eat Baked Alaska (desire), but if have neither the recipe nor the necessary ingredients (demands), Jones will eat pretzels again tonight.

Desire-oriented seminars hold as their main goal the ideal life and work backwards to see what obstacles are in the way of getting there. Demand-oriented seminars spend much of their energy on the obstacles without a clear understanding of why we are navigating the obstacle. Both types have value but are even more powerful when combined.

Our society today screams, "You can do it all!" If we don't we are a failure. Merely working through the filing techniques, memory exercises, and to-do lists in today's busy world is like lifting your feet out of a hole along the beach. If you merely lift your feet to expose an opening (i.e. increased amount of time for use somewhere else), the waves quickly fill the void just as some new responsibility or task will quickly absorb excess time. When we combine demand and desire, we are not simply lifting our feet. We are stopping to build a barrier wall around our feet so that when we lift them the waves cannot close the hole, just as striving for a better life prevents other demands from filling our precious time.

Sacrifice

A final reason that I may be just a trifle over-exuberant when presenting a seminar on time management is my desire to help other people understand the need to sacrifice, a word I rarely hear used in today's conversations. It implies a failure to obtain everything we want or suggests we must give up something for something else. This is America, the land of opportunity. We should be able to work as hard as we want, and the end result be a utopian lifestyle. Perhaps if we had the ideal job, ideal coworkers, ideal friends, and ideal family members, coupled with ideal circumstances, that would be a possibility. We do not, however, and something must be scaled back in order to obtain something else.

Writing this book was a task like I had never tackled before. I had endured graduate school, marriage, and child rearing, but was unprepared for the mental focus it would take to put meaningful words on paper in such a way that they had value to others. For a while I tried to put in an hour here and there, thinking that in a few weeks I would be done. That 60 or 120 minutes turned out to be little more than cranking the mental engine, only to shut it off a few moments later without even getting out of the driveway. My schedule would not allow me to put more into the effort, and my time with Lisa and Alex is something on which I do not compromise if possible.

My solution was not one I particularly liked. I began getting up at 5:00 AM each morning and working for about three hours on nothing but the book. Regardless of the time I went to bed, I got up at 5:00 AM. There were mornings when I would have given any amount of money to just sleep for a few minutes longer. One morning I actually reached for my glasses from the nightstand and fell asleep with my arm propped on the nightstand. I was one tired unit. Once I got up, however, I was fine and my thoughts flowed freely.

The additional sleep would have been nice, but the completed book is much better (based upon your purchase and reading to this point). Sacrifice is a seemingly necessary evil that can bring much reward if the right things are sacrificed. Too often, however, the wrong things are minimized to make way for ones that are not as important in our values inventory (see Values). Parents who both work to achieve career success and financial well being but sacrifice their children's development in the process are an example. Recently, a British au pair (similar to a nanny) was charged with manslaughter for the death of a small child of two working parents. Before the case came to trial, an article in a local newspaper took an interesting angle with the situation. The writer stated that the parents were as much to blame as the nanny. Her reasoning was that the parents had entrusted the care of a small child for ten or twelve hours per day to a woman less than twenty years old. Her article questioned the reasoning of two successful doctors who obviously did not both have to work to make ends meet. Her take was that they wanted all the elements of a complete life without all the responsibility. If children were going to be such a drag on their lifestyle that they needed to employ a full time caregiver for him, perhaps they should have waited until they were willing to make the sacrifices necessary to provide a better home for the child. Sacrifice that which is of less importance to devote more time to that which is more important.

Where to Begin

Recreating the environment necessary for a willingness to change is not necessary within the confines of this book. Grabbing someone by their emotional collar and helping them see a need to change course is best accomplished by talking face to face. From this point forward we will focus on five areas: choosing the right house, reviewing the blueprint, hiring contractors who understand your blueprint, meeting with the contractors, and paying the mortgage.

Choosing the Right House

When I was in college, I wanted a two-story white wood house with black shutters and an upstairs porch accessible only from the master bedroom. I am not there yet but am working toward the goal. What's that? You say that house style does not interest you? Okay, what is your home of preference? A brick ranch? Maybe a log home? Whatever the case, before we actually begin the process of managing our time, we must first create the desire to do so. Ask yourself these questions:

> *What is the ideal life and/or job situation for me in five*
> *years?*
> *Am I completing the steps necessary to get there?*

What other steps have not been taken?
Armed with our responses, we can proceed with Step 2 because we now have a reason to better manage our time resources.

Review the Blueprint

When you have chosen the ideal house style, the next step is to develop a blueprint. You should have definite ideas about how large the living room will be or how much closet space the bedrooms will contain. There will have to be give and take or the house could cost you an even larger fortune.

Once we have our personal vision of utopia, we have to determine the foundations upon which we will build it. Will friendships be an important part? What about the give and take of career versus family? Answers to these and similar questions will pop up more than once in your quest for the best in life. Our personal blueprint is our values, those things that we show as important by expending our mental physical, emotional, financial, and spiritual energies on them. For a more in-depth discussion of values and values clarification, turn to the values chapter before continuing on in our one on one time-management seminar.

Hiring Contractors Who Understand Your Blueprint

Let's suppose your home of choice is a log home. To choose a builder you break out the yellow pages and pick the first one on the list, right? Maybe your friend who has a stucco home can recommend his builder. Sarcasm not withstanding, you would research several builders who are familiar with log homes and ask to see examples of their work. Quality materials and workmanship should be of utmost concern as long as they fell within your loan constraints.

As we edge closer to what we do on a daily basis to make the most of our time, we cannot leapfrog the step of setting goals that match up with our values and search for a better life. They are the mental road map by which we will plan our daily direction.

Meet with the Contractors

Our house is taking shape. The foundation is laid, the walls are up, and the roof is in place. The tough part is over. You can rest assured that even without ever stepping into your new home until it is completed, everything will be perfect. Right? Now only the interior walls, electrical wiring, fixtures, appliances, plumbing, floor covering, windows, and a few thousand other details demand attention. Even with the proper foundations in place, your house will be little more than a bad dream if the chimney does not work, the washer is in the wrong place, or the expensive ceiling molding is mistakenly used in the closets. Clearly, if ever there was a time to pay close attention to every detail, it would be in this phase.

This is the point at which many seminars begin…The daily planning element. With our background information you have the added benefit of understanding the larger reason behind getting the things done that are important to you.

A host of time management seminars offer varying ways to accomplish the task of itemizing your daily list of things to do. In my time management seminars I give several examples, but offer only one here for illustration.

Make a list of everything you would like to accomplish today, including tasks that are not urgent. If you had thought about walking to get some much-needed exercise, write it down. The key here is to get it all (or as much as possible) down on paper. Holding your tasks in your head because you think you can recall the items later is an exercise in futility.

Take a deck of cards. For each item you need to write down, get a card from the stack. Once you have exhausted your list of things to do, add another five to seven cards for things that will crop up during the day. Now take those cards and construct a card house like you did when you were younger. The catch is that you can only have four cards as your vertical base for the home. The remainder must be built on that base. Tricky, huh? If you do get it built, imagine that I told you I needed you to move it to another table. Crash!

Our memories work in much the same manner. We stack more and more things in it, thinking we can quickly recall them when necessary. That works fine when we have a few items and our mental house seems to be in order. Keep adding items to your memory, however (more cards to the house), and soon it crashes, throwing items everywhere. It's called sending your mind to the hereafter. Ever walk into a room and wonder, "What did I come in here after?" One of the key causes for it is that we constantly pack so many items into our brain that it gives up on trying to recall them. Writing things down that you want and need to do helps insure that your mind can function properly and focus on matters at hand instead of consistently grappling to hold on to a thought that could be lost in the stack.

The second step is to give a value to each item. The most common system uses A B C, where A is most important. These tasks should be tackled or scheduled first. B represents activities that should be done. The world will not stop if they are not done, but they will need our attention soon. C stands for items that are trivial. These items can be done if the A and B ones are completed and will be considered icing on the time-management cake if they are done today.

Where to Put All This Stuff

Congratulations on reaching this point. You have made it further than most people ever do. Our task is now to determine where to put this set of directions for our day. Common places I have seen others use include a note card, sticky note, or the back of their hand. Legal pads, scrap paper, or a napkin are a few other places to inscribe a list of things to do. These places are less than acceptable, however, when you struggle with where to keep that sticky note or napkin so it will be in your plain view and available for immediate retrieval.

Enter the planner. My only regret with planners is that I did not invest in the stock of companies that produce these delightful tools. I could then have dictated this book to someone else to type and organize into a readable document. Planners are wonderful in that they offer a place to maintain daily lists and keep up with a world of other information that may be needed from time to time. Planners are sold in office supply stores and discount retailers and through mail order. Each offers its own bells and whistles, but I have found none to be perfect (be my investment source and we will make one that is perfect). Instead, each planner will have to be customized to fit your specific needs. For me, an effective planner has the following components:

- Ring binder: This makes it easy to insert or remove pages when necessary.

- Daily List Space: You can write your list here and have it in a secure location.

- Daily journal: Record any pertinent information here such as phone calls, notes from a meeting, conversations, or bright ideas (I know you have them).

- Monthly calendars: Make sure they have enough space to write appointments or commitments.

- Telephone/Address List: Keeping your address/telephone list separate from your planner or daily list is disastrous. Many commitments include calling someone or sending them information via fax, e mail, or US Mail.

- Values/Goals: Having these in your planner can help you get back on track if things seem to be going haywire around you.

Tips On Making Effective Use Of A Planner

Take your planner with you everywhere. I tell audiences that the only place I do not take my planner is into the shower and to church. I should take it to church because I get asked about my availability for meetings on a regular basis. How many times have you been visiting friends who ask you about going to a sporting event or community activity on a certain date? Not having your planner with you, you promise to call them when you get home after checking your calendar. You forget about it when you arrive home and do not call them for a few days. You remember it when their names are mentioned in conversation with your spouse, and you rush to the phone to tell them you are available. Too late. They gave the tickets to someone else. Having your planner with you enables you to take care of matters at hand now.

Use only one calendar. On your refrigerator there is probably a calendar from a church or civic organization next to a child's school and/or sports schedule. At work you have a calendar on your desk, and your spouse has a similar one in their office. Add a planner to the mix, and things get really interesting. Each time you consider committing to an obligation, you run the equivalent of the Boston Marathon, checking dates and availability on all the calendars.

While it may be impossible to down size to one calendar, you should be able to reduce the number of them. A large family calendar at home in a prominent location, combined with a planner for each spouse, should suffice in most cases. As you get other schedules or calendars, write important dates on the family calendar and in your personal planner.

Paying the Mortgage

Having completed your home, you enjoy the first fruits of your labor as you build a fire in the fireplace and sit together with your family in front of the glowing embers. Life, at this moment, is wonderful. Unfortunately, the bliss is temporary. Your hand soon reaches into your mailbox, and in the mass of sales papers and credit card applications you find a mortgage book from a lending institution. Whether by bank draft or actual payment coupons, we now have the obligation to make regular payments to pay off our debt.

Having the ideal life in mind, setting appropriate goals and proper planning with a planner will only get you so far in the pursuit of happiness. The final component is the things you do on a daily basis that offer the greatest return on investment. Here is a list of tips and strategies that may help in reducing the debt of time that we so often sense in our daily activities.

- Write It Down! I say again, "Write it down!" Stop trying to hold thoughts, ideas or important commitments in your mind. Get them on paper so your mind can focus on the matters of the moment.

- Find Your Peak Performance Time. When are you most mentally awake? For me it is first thing in the morning. I have friends, though, whose minds do not get beyond understanding the time of day until noon. They typically are most mentally productive late at night. The follow-up question is, "What are you doing when you are most mentally awake?" In other words, does the mental or physical requirement needed for a task match your mental or physical alertness of the moment? Granted, we can not tell our boss that we will be in three hours late because we are mentally stimulated in the morning and want to complete a high mental activity. Nevertheless, forcing ourselves to do activities that do not match our mental or physical capabilities of the moment is a frequent source of stress and frustration. Reading an in-depth business report at 7:00 PM may seem necessary because you have to know the facts by noon tomorrow, but if your mental capacity has been drained by the experiences of the day, then you may spend two hours on a task that would take you fifteen minutes at a more appropriate time. Find your peak performance time for mental and physical activities, and try to match the appropriate activities with them

- Ask yourself, "Would anything terrible happen if I did not do this item?" If not, then don't do it. Straightening your desk or filing those papers may seem like a priority, but if you feel stressed out because of more pressing items, these may be postponed for a few days.

- Delegate, Delegate, Delegate. Okay, so maybe the other person will not do the stellar job you would do with the task. However, is there something more important on which you could concentrate if someone else completed the task?

- Chop the Tree Down a Limb or Two at a Time. When attempting a less than desirable task, work on the most important and difficult parts first. Set aside a window of time to focus on only that task, allowing yourself the flexibility to continue with it if you get into a rhythm or on a roll. Many times once we finally get started, the task does not seem so monumental. That is doubly so if we succeed at the most challenging portion first.

Summing It Up

One of my favorite phrases is "As the want gets stronger, the how gets easier." Building a time-management plan from the standpoint of what you want to accomplish or get out of your time resources is critical. History is full of people who wanted something so desperately that they found a way to get it. Simply looking for quick tips may help us be more productive during a day, but our goal is to be productive not only that day but over a lifetime. Whether it is a house, relationship, or legacy, our passion to reach the important things must be evident in each and every activity we undertake.

U

Unity (Teamwork)

Surprisingly enough, I find myself practically speechless as I reach this chapter. Although I have a wealth of information and thoughts on being a good team member, I find much of it contained within other chapters. A similar scenario took place a few years ago when I developed a training manual for a youth organization. It had all the regular chapters on self-esteem, team building, and similar topics. When I got to the requested chapter on leadership, I drew a blank. If these young people implemented many of these concepts into their year as an officer, they would be exhibiting leadership of the most excellent kind.

Based upon my premise that many of the elements of an effective team are contained elsewhere in this book, I will refrain from repeating myself. My brief dissertation on team work can be condensed into six suggestions:

1) Develop a standard of beliefs as a team. One of the biggest downfalls of any team is that a member does something that is viewed as inappropriate by the other team members but is not spelled out in any way. Animosity develops because the person or persons feel like they are being held to a different standard than the other officers. Extreme behaviors, such as physical abuse of another person, stealing, or abandoning your duties may constitute clear grounds for dismissal, but what are the expectations or standards of excellence each member is expected to adhere to? Developing a standard of beliefs helps remove most emotional confrontations that arise from a perception of unfair treatment.

2) Spend quality time with each other. Yes, I said quality time. Schedule time to do nothing except enjoy the company of the other members of the group/team. Make it a rule that no one can discuss "business," and instead conversations must focus on who you are as individuals.

3) Make your conversations more than a request. On one of my teams is a person who only calls when they want something from me related to our professional relationship. Business must be transacted, but always making my need for conversation and friendship second to his need for information has created a stale relationship that does not look out for the best interests of each member...another key facet of a successful team.

4) See the value in every player. Make a conscious effort to learn and appreciate the strengths of every member of your team. Just because one person's talent seems more important than another, do not discount the worth of someone else. The center on a basketball team may perform a wonderful dunk while in mid air, but without the pass from the guard his moment would never be realized. Appreciating each person's abilities also serves to minimize jealousy, another weak link in a successful team.

5) Celebrate each person's identity. Be positive about their life, and cheer them on when they are attempting things outside their role as a team player. Knowing that you care about them as an individual makes them trust you that much more when on the team.

6) Practice, Practice, Practice. One of my favorite parts of a leadership conference is conducting activities designed to encourage teamwork. The fact that people can be at each other's throat one moment and high-fiving each other the next shows great growth. Through such exercises they will find ways to appreciate each other and ultimately transfer that understanding to working together in their official capacity.

A Final Thought

With those suggestions in mind, examine how your team measures up. More importantly, determine how you measure up to the standards here. Few teams have individuals who will consistently respond in such a way that shows that they have the group's best interest at heart. As we have discussed in earlier chapters (resolving conflict, building bridges, optical illusions and personality) it is extremely difficult, if not impossible, to control the thoughts and/or actions of someone else. No matter how hard we may try to control them, the other person or persons have their own agendas and perceptions which are deeply ingrained into their personality. Hopefully, utilizing the strategies and ideas offered in other chapters of this book will assist you in beginning the process of more effective cooperation.

Perhaps the most effective way, however, to teach your fellow team members about the importance of working together is to be a good team member yourself. Like the quotation, if you want a friend, be one, if you want a great team, be a great team member.

V

Values

If you have read this book from the beginning to this point, you are aware of all the chapters that have made reference to this one: Character, Decisions, Goals, Nuptials, Quality vs. Quantity Time, and Time Management. Accident? Afraid not. Beyond the readily visible features of a successful person (i.e. image, abilities, personality) lies something more difficult to explain with mere words. It is like describing the wind. We cannot explain what the wind is, but we can explain what its effect is on us and our surroundings. Our values are like the wind. They have an effect, either good or bad, on the people and things around us.

We all have values. We may lack morals or character, but we *all* have those things that we deem as worthy of our energy. The former generation tells the latter generation that their values are changing, and the latter screams back that they need to get a life and move into their shoes for awhile.

If character can be defined as "Who are you when no one is looking?" values might be defined as "What do your actions say about who you are, regardless of who is looking?" Our values become much like character cash, which we spend on those things that we believe to have great worth. Based on those expenditures, others can look at our internal ledger sheet to determine our values. Spend an exorbitant amount in one area, and there is no way to deny our allegiance to that relationship, career, or even material item.

Identifying our values, then, would seem to simply be an exercise in looking at where we spend our energy. The frustrating part of that, however, is that many times it is scary when we dissect our daily routines. We see that much of our character cash is being embezzled by one area of our life while another area is scraping to get by.

Let's use the classic example of a teenager for a moment. Young people in their teens place a premium on the value of their friendships and acceptance within social circles, so much so that they are willing to spend less on their family and education to invest more in their friends. Family relationships frequently become strained because a parent's values have not changed; as they still hold their son/daughter as one of the most important things in their life. They feel cheated in some respects because the child has given them second class status in their life.

As we grow older, our values evolve with us. If anyone had told me at the age of 16 that the value of good health would outweigh (bad choice of words) the value of financial success, I would have scoffed at them. At 31, however, having seen my dad suffer through open heart surgery, along with several blood relatives who have had heart problems, it has become all too clear that financial success means little if you are dead. Jobs are a premium in the lives of many people. Giving them too much worth, however, causes strains within a marriage that sometimes lead to separation or divorce. This reality check forces the person to examine their values and to rearrange them in order to save the relationship.

The true worth of determining our values, then, is not so much to correct problems that exist in our current situation (although it can), but rather to decide who or what gets our resources and in what order. We do it subconsciously every day. Actually writing them down helps us to make espousing them a more conscious activity.

Getting Started

Break out a pen and a piece of paper. You can write in this book but then allowing someone to borrow it might bare your soul more than you wish. Begin with this question:

"If someone were a silent observer of you for a period of two weeks, what would they say you value, based on your actions?"

The key here is "based on your actions." We can reason away why we did not do something and feel okay with ourselves. A silent observer, however, would hear nothing from you and only watch your expenditure of energy.

When Lisa was researching the steps to writing and publishing a book, Lisa found many materials to assist with the process. One of the most enlightening was a chapter in a book explaining the proofreading process. Their instructions were to give it to someone who would not patronize you or your work and would give an objective appraisal. They additionally commented that you should simply hand the manuscript to them, without making excuses. Their rationale was that there would be no place in the book for a verbal or written disclaimer telling why this book was not as it should be. It would have to stand on its own since the author could not be present with each person reading the book to point out challenging sections or ones that were deficient in some way. Our values are much the same. We have to let our actions speak for themselves.

Attempting to define ourselves through the eyes of others may not be easy, but being honest is rarely ever simple. Try to focus on their comments to you. What did they talk about with you? Even more importantly, what did you talk about with them? Was it your job that hogged the conversation? Perhaps you mentioned your spouse. Maybe you told several humorous things that your two-year-old is doing. Reflect on your attitude when working in the different arenas of your three-ring circus. Would that silent observer see a person in contempt of their career choice. Perhaps they would they see your children longing to see more of you?

Taking it a step further, let us suppose your silent observer saw you pass from this life. Who would miss you the most? Why? Is it because of your value to them or is it because they wanted so much more but never got much of your quantity or quality time? Your silent observer is now passing through the crowd (hopefully) gathered to mourn your death. What will they hear others say about you?

If you have not already made the connection with time management, let me plug it in for you. My underlying passion with respect to time is that we have no choice but to proactively invest in those areas of our life of greatest importance, deemed important by our intellectual and heart-felt thoughts *now* instead of an emotional explosion that forces us to pick up the pieces and rebuild again later. Unfortunately, death allows no time for picking up the pieces, especially if that death is ours.

Having that list in hand, let us travel to the other side (of the emotional fence, that is). Ask yourself this question: "What do I want to value in my life?" Remember our definition of value: Those persons, ideals, or things to which you will spend your physical, mental, emotional and financial energy. At this point, don't worry about ranking or describing them. Just write your list. It may include your obvious roles as spouse, parent, or employee, but it may also include ideals like believing in others or being honest.

With your two lists in hand, make a comparison/contrast (I always hated those assignments in English class). How well do they match? If you are like most people, the less well they match, the more stress you feel in your life. Even if it is a temporary situation, a gap between our desired values and those of our daily efforts can be destructive.

Lisa and I have one of the most unique relationships I know. In our seven years of marriage we have grown interdependent like I never imagined. We compliment each other. While other marriages have fallen down around us, ours has only grown stronger. Even so, there are those times when my values have gotten a little out of whack. One Friday night I returned from an errand to find Lisa was playing in the floor with Alex. As she looked up at me, I sensed that there was something amiss. When I asked her, the response was "nothing." (We will discuss that further in the xy chapter.) Inquiring further, she said, "We *never* go out as a couple. I love Alex to death, but sometimes I just want to be with you for a little while." Thinking back over the previous eight weeks, I could not recall a time that Lisa and I had been alone together for more than two hours. I had been placing a much greater value on my job and on being a good father than on being a good spouse. The difficult part was that I could not change it at that moment. The next several day's commitments were already in place, and things could not be changed. I did, however, make plans for the following week.

Just telling her I would do something about it means little beyond her trust in me. It was only when I actually opened her car door and escorted her to the movies or the restaurant or just to a quiet place that she would know that I was adjusting my values. Too many relationships are held together by the string of "I will try to do better," only to have that string worn down over time because we never actually do anything to improve the situation. People lose their jobs because of an unwillingness to put actions behind the phrase, "I will do better."

If the gap between the items in your list of perceptions and realities is large you may want to examine how you can bring the two lists more in line with each other. It will not be easy, but remember, "As the want gets stronger, the how gets easier." One way to begin the process of reconciliation and getting back on your values track is to describe how you can reinforce each value in your daily efforts. What are the things you can do to exemplify those values? Regardless of the value, I sincerely believe that we can find concrete ways to show that the particular area has worth in our life. In fact, we already do it without realizing it.

Finally, we must put these values with descriptions into a defined order of importance. Even with all the grunt work of crystallizing our values and describing how we will exemplify them, they mean little if we can not use them as a source for our decisions and goals.

One of my best friends in high school had a magnificent career opportunity about eighteen months ago. He would be the director for a camp and conference center. The flexibility of the job was extraordinary and his talents would no doubt have the center growing by leaps and bounds. He uprooted his family and moved, making quick strides toward improvement of the center.

Recently, I heard through my parents that he was resigning from the position. Apparently his wife had been unhappy with the living conditions of the family. Having seen the conditions, I fully understand. Knowing how much my friend wanted to succeed in the position, I felt, at first a great loss for him. Thinking beyond the obvious, though, I realized that he had done what few people are willing to do: Live by their values. His desire for the happiness of his wife far outweighed his drive to be successful in his current career choice. Ranking our values is actually not the most difficult step. Abiding by the order is the tough part. Doing so, however, gives us the ability to have peace within ourselves because we are spending our energies in a manner that shows worth to our relationships, ideals, and philsophies.

As for ranking your values, a simple process seems in order. Take each value listed on your sheet and write it on a slip of paper (haven't we been here before?). Place them in front of you. Ask yourself, "If my energy bank account had to cease paying benefits to one thing, what would it be?" Continue the process until you have done it with all your values. The first few are simple, while the last few will be the subject of much frustration. You will scream at this book, saying, "But they are both important!" Yes they are, but if your resources were such that you could only pay benefits to one thing, what one thing would you pay?

Keep your final list with its rank order and descriptions. I keep my list in my planner and reflect on it from time to time. Especially in times of high stress (low resources), the list helps me to reexamine what those things are that I give the most value to and how I have chosen to express them. It becomes a sort of mental report card, except that I get to grade myself.

Wrapping It Up

Pardon me while I put away my soap box again. When she was proofreading the book, Lisa said it was easy to tell which chapters I was most passionate about. This was one she highlighted. It just seems to me that as a society we have taken an approach of self-denial in respect to our values. We are afraid to reflect on who we are for fear of what we might see. Additionally, we do not want to dig too deeply, for to do so might uncover a person very different from the one on the surface. Ultimately, we seem to refrain from planting our values in good soil for fear of having to actually work to bring them to full bloom. It just seems easier to go with the flow.

I close this chapter with something very personal. Written below are a few of my values as a person. This is not an inclusive list, but is offered merely as a guide as you develop your own.

I have a successful marriage. I spend quality time with my wife and am attentive to her needs, problems and feelings. I work constantly for the good of "us" and am not afraid to sacrifice my needs for our needs.

I believe in others. I commit a portion of my day to keeping in touch with my friends and relatives. I see each individual as having worth and seek to encourage their growth as a person. I realize that I am no better than anyone else but am simply a tool to be used wonderfully by God. I honor commitments I have made to them.

I am a healthy person. I exercise regularly and keep my weight within a prescribed range. I additionally eat the proper foods and refrain from poor dietary habits.

I am a financially successful individual. We operate on an income that meets our needs and offers the opportunities for wants to be met on a planned basis. My wife is free to do the work she most enjoys without being concerned with the monetary implications of not receiving constant income. Our child will need for nothing but will learn the value of responsibility and sound financial management.

This is not an inclusive list, but is offered merely as a guide as you develop your own. The key is to attempt to explain them in concrete terms that offer a blueprint for your actions on a daily basis. You may find that once you have described your values, it becomes easier to plan your response to life's situations or obstacles. Adhering to your own values offers the opportunity to enjoy the inner peace of knowing that people will rarely be confused by a discrepancy between your words and your actions. Ultimately, you might even find that life itself has greater value.

Wisdom

The word wisdom in our language comes from the Greek word "sophia." Clement of Alexandria (early Greek history) defines it as "the knowledge of things human and divine and of their causes." Aristotle described it as "striving after the best ends and using the best means." Today's dictionaries use words like enlightened or wise to illuminate the word. Regardless of your own personal defining of the word, wisdom is something we all possess, though we normally associate it most with experienced people (notice I did not say old) or those who have suffered much adversity in life. "You are wise beyond your years" is a common phrase.

The idea that only elder statesman know the best ends and means to a successful life was challenged just a few years ago. A father, preparing for the departure of his son to college, wrote a list of phrases and brief sentences that he thought would be helpful to his child when entering the real world. They covered everything from purchasing practices to spiritual stability. Encouraged by his peers and his son, the man published the list into a little "Instruction Book." Soon after, an avalanche of books hit the shelves that offered morsels of motivational thought about understanding the means to get the most out of life. One of my favorite books noted the age of the persons from whom the quotations were taken. They ranged in age from 6 to 106.

What struck me was the fact that the wisdom of the younger ones rivaled the quality of their more experienced elders.

We all have wisdom to impart to others. Irrespective of age, creed, or gender, everyone understands some facet of life and the way to strive for the best in it. We just seem to focus on those who have been around longer and who are more successful. "They have based it on the anvil of experience," we say. What about learning the wisdom of things from those who have not been successful? Much can be learned about how to have a successful marriage by listening to the pain-filled words of someone experiencing a divorce. Lisa and I look to parents with model children to tell us the roots of successful child rearing but have caught ourselves lending an ear to the frazzled parent of a holy terror just as often. For success in my line of work, I learn as much from viewing those who are struggling as I do from the ones immensely popular on the speaking circuit.

As individuals, most of us do not like to say we are wise in the sense discussed here. To do so would cause people to watch us to see if our immortal words are reflected in our own lives. Strangely enough, whether we like it or not, they are watching us already. Parents do not have to tell children to follow their example...they will anyway in many cases. Get a job as a manager, and all those around you will watch to see your skills and talents expressed in your communications with your employees. It does not have to be verbally expressed. Unlike the movie *Forrest Gump,* in which the lead character often repeated, "Mama always said," we know that people learn from our examples as much as they do from external exhortations.

The remainder of this chapter includes wisdom from my own life experiences. Some observations are my own while others I have picked up from speeches, conversations, or some other medium. I share these not out of a sense of being superior to anyone but as a way of thanking those whose wisdom has brought me this far in life. Additionally, I hope that it stimulates your own thinking about the marvelous wisdom represented by your own life. In fact, many of the tidbits shared here were learned more from family, neighbors, and friends than they were from any great orator or person of high education. Some require explanation while others speak more when they are not explained. Ultimately, I encourage you to write your own list and add to it often. Who knows, someone may ask you to put them into a book one day.

As we see people we treat them, and as we treat them they become.

Mamie McCollough, a motivational speaker, shared this idea in a speech a few years ago, and it has been a guiding principle for me ever since. Think about it for a moment. As a teacher, I have had many students who were not perfect. I found that if I saw them as having little potential to learn and treated them that way, they would become people of little potential because I did not give them a fair chance. On the other hand, if I attempted to see them as having some great ability waiting to reveal itself and treated them that way, they would rise to my expectations and usually even surpass them.

Of course, the relationship is not directly proportional. Just because I see someone as easy to work with does not mean that there will not be many tense moments and discussions. Using my premise as a way to treat them and respond to them, however, goes much further toward developing a successful relationship than seeing them as an impossible individual.

As the want gets stronger, the how gets easier.

Each time I find myself listing a hundred reasons why something cannot be done, I stop and ask myself, "Do I really want to do it?" If not, then the search focuses on reasons for my unwillingness to engage the task. If the answer is yes, then my focus becomes doing something to make the decision a reality. Organizations could save themselves much misery if, in the heat of a debate about the best way to do something, someone would call time out and say, "Do we really want to do this?" If the answer is yes, proceed. If the answer is no, then perhaps they should dig for reasons why there is resistance to implementing a new direction.

We make a decision and we make it right.

Relatively few decisions in our lives are simple. Rather they are a complex maze of unknowns, uncertainties, and insecurities. Just making the decision is one step; *implementing* it is another. I can make the decision to get married and then do nothing to make the marriage work. A few years later the relationship ends in divorce, and I wrongfully reason, "It just was not meant to be" or "It was a bad decision." Granted, the person you chose may not have been a model spouse, but what did you do to make the initial decision a correct one? A concept similar to this one is, "People stop looking for work when they get a job." Just getting the chance at employment is one thing. Doing the things to make the occupation a success is another.

A ship in harbor is safe, but that is not what ships are made for.

Going outside our comfort zone is scary, and offers numerous opportunities for failure, ridicule, and even physical or emotional pain. To reach our fullest potential, however, we have to go out on the high seas of uncertainty, knowing that our relationships, skills, and quest for life's best will keep us afloat regardless of the outcome.

Excel, then evaluate.

Because we desire instant gratification, we quickly attempt a new career or task. If things do not immediately reach our level of satisfaction (and they rarely do), we return to our old way of doing things, certain it was not meant to be. Instead of retreating so readily, we should instead make a genuine, sincere effort to be successful by giving the career or task sufficient time. Doing so gives us a more correct scale on which to evaluate its progress.

Force is not the answer.

A student in my class had a terrible temper. Not with people, but with things. When constructing or repairing something, he would quickly grow impatient that things did not proceed at the rate he desired. His solution was to beat it with a hammer, kick it, or force a part to fit in area that it was definitely not made for.

Many of us go through life much the same way. If a situation does not go the way we planned, we believe yelling, banging on something, or belittling someone will get results. It is true that in a number of cases the "squeaky wheel gets the grease," but approaching every conflict or obstacle with that attitude only serves to infuriate other individuals involved or destroy someone or something.

We recently had a problem with the phone lines near our home. Every time it rained the lines would short out, and the phones would go dead. Usually, the problem would last 16 to 24 hours. If you work out of a home office, you can imagine my frustration. I tried all the usual channels from screaming at a customer service representative to threatening to change local service providers. They would send out a lineman who would fix the short, but that was only a short-term solution. Finally, I wrote a letter of complaint to the phone company and sent a copy to the state utilities commission. I got a call three days later from the regional vice president and the local repair manager. Twenty-four hours after those calls the problem was fixed. In addition, I got a $125 credit on my phone bill and a personal number to call if I had any further problems. Force is not always the answer. Showing a degree of intelligence may be part of a better solution.

Be passionate about something other than yourself.

Whether it is a relationship, a charitable organization, or a belief, devote so much energy to it that you can take pride (the good kind) in a job well done.

If you have a happy family, you are successful.

While attending a function a few years ago, I had the opportunity to talk with a rare gentleman. I was soon to be out of college and in the real world. As he was listening to my grand plans, he stopped me in mid-sentence and asked me, "That's great…but how do you define success?" My fumbled answer showed that I did not have a clear handle on my thoughts. In his response he talked about all the career moves he was offered but turned down because it would have had a negative impact on his family. "I can find another job," he said, "but I cannot find another family." "Even worse," he continued, "is the fact that if I do a lousy job with my family, I have affected generations to come." He died six months later. In visiting with the family, I sensed that while they greatly missed him, they took great comfort in knowing that this man had made the happiness of his family his most important priority.

The pain of discipline and commitment is measured in ounces. The pain of regret and disappointment is measured in tons.

People with no dreams will seek to destroy yours.

It is impossible to create vision within others if you have none yourself.

Make the quality of your life visual, not verbal.

People will never care how much you know until they know how much you care.

Men and Women

Yes, I cheated by combining two letters in one chapter. But they made such a cute couple (Get it? men... women... couple?) Originally, they were going to be separate, but with the biological significance of the two letters, I thought it would work better this way. Actually, I could not see myself attempting to write a chapter on understanding women without relating it to the way a man thinks for comparison.

Men and women are different. Big news flash, huh? Although we have more jokes about the opposite sex than any other area of our lives, an intelligent being will tell you we desperately need the combination of man and woman to be whole or complete. Like any other relationship, however, we have to appreciate the differences we possess instead of seeing them as stumbling blocks.

While this topic intrigues me from a practical standpoint (team building, conflict resolution, etc.), I have to admit that I get a great deal of warped joy out of watching men and women try to get along. One of my most requested programs for evenings of pure entertainment is a humorous collection of the ways the sexes differ and how to live in a more harmonious environment. I sincerely hope that you enjoy the following thoughts as much as I do sharing them with a group. While a major basis of these comments is marriage, the concepts introduced can assist in improving professional relationships in the work place or friendships.

Men look at life practically, while women see details and how to add beauty to things. A natural place to test this is in our shopping styles. A man is practical, and if he wants to shop for a pair of shoes, he sets his homing device on shoes. You can shop with him anywhere you want, but he will have only one thing on his mind-getting the shoes. You'll find a similar situation if you send a man in to get a loaf of bread and a gallon of milk. He will return with a loaf of bread and a gallon of milk.

A woman, on the other hand, likes to browse when shopping because she is thinking about more than immediate needs. She may walk into the store saying she is shopping for shoes, but a few minutes later she can be found in the fabrics, housewares, or even the garden area. The man will say, "I thought you came in here to look at shoes." She will reply, "I did, but I was thinking about redecorating the bathroom and wanted to look at some material for curtains." A similar situation arises when we return to the grocery store. The woman who was sent in for a loaf of bread and a gallon of milk will return with two or three bags of groceries. Why? While she was shopping, she remembered that she needed items to bake a cake for a weekend outing or had a coupon for coffee that was about to expire. Women look beyond the basic needs of the moment.

How do we deal with this difference? When shopping, women have learned that you take the man to all the other shopping locations first and then to his desired destination last. Using this approach prevents him from getting what he wants first and then moaning about being ready to return home as soon as possible, the need for shopping over in his mind. On the other side, men have learned to give women a defined time to shop in order to be somewhere else. Another tool used by many men if they have to go shopping with a woman is to plan it around a meal time. At least then they get the satisfaction of having a meal along with the drudgery of shopping.

Looking at this difference on a grander scale, you will discover some definite strategies to implement when attempting to plan activities or work with the opposite sex. Men have to be frequently reminded of the larger picture and that not everyone thinks like they do. Women, on the contrary, have to focus their thoughts in a more concise manner. Giving too much information or expressing too many ideas only serves to confuse the man who is attempting to hone in on one or two main points.

Men report while women discuss. Men talk to report new information while women want to express their feelings and analyze the situation. A prime example is apparent in our TV viewing habits. Women want TV shows with a plot like a romance or suspense thriller. Men, however, like action movies where something happens, and then they can move on to something else. Men love newspapers because they are chock full of new information. When Lisa and I sit down to look at the morning paper, we never have to fight over who gets what section. I want the A section with all the stories of events around the world while Lisa wants the Living Section or similar part with *Dear Abby* and other more involved articles.

If you are still not convinced of this morsel of magnificent wisdom, try this experiment. Ask your spouse, significant other or coworker of the opposite sex, "How was your day?" The men will respond by telling you what they did, where they went, and whom they saw. New information. Women will talk about situations, people's feelings, and their own feelings toward a predicament at work or another person. One writer explained men's fascination with new information as originating in caveman days. Men would return to the cave exclaiming, "Me got 3 rabbits for supper!" Of course, the cave woman probably replied, "Me not going to cook those nasty things... me want to go out!"

As a foundation for working together, women need to remember that men do not talk much because they report what they know and stop. They will talk again when there is new information to be analyzed or dispersed. A woman may need to put a new twist on an old argument or approach it from a different angle to renew the man's interest in the subject. From a man's vantage point, he will need to relax and realize that the woman is thinking out loud and is not just reporting new information. Having shared her innermost thoughts, she will alert you to the fact she is ready for an answer.

Another wedge causing conflict between the sexes in regards to communication is the man's desire to fix stuff while the woman wants to just think out loud. In our early days of teaching Lisa would come home telling of her frustrations or disappointments of the day. Being the male and Mr. Fix-it, I would usually give some type of response about how to repair the situations. Lisa would be very patient, but I could tell that she was uneasy with me. Eventually, after she had heard all she could stand, she would respond, "You just have an answer for everything." Men have been taught to fix things all their lives, and they carry that over to their discussions on more abstract matters. Women like to share their ups and downs because it creates a type of bond with the person with whom she is sharing. Just having the comfort of a shoulder to lean on often gives a woman the self-confidence necessary to make a decision on her own. Demanding answers to their thoughts at every opportunity only makes them feel inadequate and incapable of making decisions on their own.

Men see life as a list of things to do while women see life as a novel to be written. At some point a wife has made the comment, "What a lovely house," while driving with the husband. Men like to see things in list form, and the wife has just created a sense of failure within the man because she has added something to his list that was not there before. The husband then begins thinking about how much money his wife spends on her hobbies or clothes. He soon lashes back at her about how they could have a nice house if she was not so monetarily wasteful. The wife, receiving a verbal slap in the face, now either retreats to her own little world or returns fire with a comment about his own spending habits.

Ironically, all the woman was doing was discussing what she saw. Women are expressive and want to respond to what they see in their environment. She probably had no thought of envy but was simply elaborating with her words on what she saw with her eyes. To prevent future situations like this from materializing, the wife may have to prod the husband, reminding him that she is just thinking out loud. If the man has a real ego problem, she may even have to make a quick positive comment to restore his damaged self-image until she can talk with him further at another time. She may have to remind him that she does not love him any less because of the smaller house in which they live. Men, on the other hand, need to realize that women are expressive and will respond to any new stimulus with a spoken word. She is most likely making no comparisons or judgements, unless your insecurity in the relationship brings you to that conclusion.

Men want to conquer. Women want security. Men get a warped thrill out of driving four hundred miles in the back woods then being able to drive up in someone's yard without a roadmap or clear directions. It is a way of conquering the unknown. Women, however, are uneasy with that and want to know exactly where they are going and how long it will take to get there. It is not that they are questioning the man's ability to drive but are simply more comfortable when they know the details.

Men love a sense of adventure and challenge. Look at the games boys play on the playground even today. They want to see who can swing the highest, run the fastest, or dethrone the guy who is king of the hill. Girls are playing games that require cooperation like jump rope or games in which winning is normally not the most important part of the activity.

Husbands have to remember that they are their wives' knights in shining armor. They are proud of their husband for taking on so many challenges to make life better for the family. Sometimes, though, the man has to get off that horse, take off the armor, and just sit and talk with his wife, letting her know that she is number one in his life. Wives need to know that every once in a while men must go out and slay a dragon or two to feel good about themselves. Sometimes, though, they may want their wives to get on that horse with them and share the joy of the unknown together.

A Final Thought

In the personality chapter I talked about how the mixture of a variety of personalities is necessary for the success of any organization. A similar thought surfaces here. Even in our era of blurring male and female roles, there is still a profound difference in the behavior of the two sexes. Only seeing these differences as grounds for confrontation or the basis for jokes, however, misses a much more important fact: *Each sex needs the other!* No, not just for reproduction, but for the marvelous complement one gender is to the other when facing pro-

fessional or personal decisions. Additionally, the power of a construc-
tive male/female relationship has been shown throughout the years to
increase the effectiveness of each person in the relationship exponen-
tially. If the X and Y chromosome can reside peacefully together on a
tiny strand of DNA and can unite with like or unlike chromosomes to
create such marvelous human beings like yourself, surely we can do as
well or better when working together in this great big world.

Z

Zeal

I always thought that when I got to this chapter I would be jumping for joy. While I am relieved to have such a monumental task almost complete, I do have a sense of fear, fear that I may never again examine my life as carefully as I have these past few months. To put into words my own philosophy of life is scary at best. With each concept introduced or strategy shared, I have a deep concern that it may not be the perfect answer to a reader's problem or situation. However, not to have shared these words at all would have been a tragedy, for we all have wisdom to impart to others. If something shared within the pages of this book sparks a new way of thinking or leads someone to get a little bit more out of life, then my time will have been well spent.

As our meal together winds down (my how time has flown), and the dinner plates are being removed, may I invite you now to partake of dessert. Following a delectable meal, a delicious dessert just seems to make everything fit together. A small piece of cheesecake with just a hint of blueberry on top would be my suggestion. Or how about a slice of sixteen-layer chocolate cake? (the layers are micro thin) Two scoops of homemade ice cream would satisfy the palate or a warm slice of apple pie ala mode would also be wonderful. I will refrain from offering some of my favorites like banana cake (not to be confused with banana nut bread) or my wife's homemade wedding cake. If I start thinking about them, this book will never get finished.

Likewise, as this book draws to a close, may I offer a suggestion for making our time together even more meaningful. May I offer you some zeal for your life? In case you have not used the word or read its definition lately, zeal is a noun meaning intense enthusiasm or intensely passionate. A zealot (when is the last time you called someone that?) is someone of intense passion or enthusiasm. I always thought it was a negative reflection on someone. Having read the definition, I now realize that people who call someone a zealot are probably just envious that they have a cause in their life that they feel so strongly about, something to which they are willing to focus so much energy. It would be my hope that we are all zealots about life and live it with intense passion. Hopefully, some of my zeal has been evident in this book.

Using all the techniques, thought processes, and strategies outlined in this book, however, will not make your life prime rib. It might create prime-rib moments, but something will always be lacking in your enthusiasm for life or your passion to make the most of every moment. It reminds me of getting a new computer for our church several years ago. Most individuals in the group had never used one, so I was the self-appointed trainer for the things we needed to do on the computer. Working with the computer programmer who set up the system, I inquired about the steps necessary to complete this task or that scenario. I painstakingly outlined each minute detail of what needed to be done. It was to be used as a flow chart for the novices in the group. Things went smoothly for the first few days, but soon my phone began to ring. "Jones, how do you...?" After making several trips to the office and enduring extended conversations on the phone trying to walk someone through the steps, I was very frustrated. Talking with my computer programmer friend again, he said, "There is a difference between knowing *about* the computer programs and *knowing* the computer programs. If you know about them, you will be okay unless a new situation arises, one in which you have not been instructed or have no flow chart to guide you. If you know the program, you can figure out what steps to take to solve your problem." To this point, this book has been a compilation of "flow charts" to guide you through many of the situations you will face (or are facing) in life. Standing alone, however, they may be limited in effectiveness, since you may have an element in your life that needs attention but is not clearly addressed by one of the topics. You may find yourself saying, "But what about how to handle…?"

As I said at the beginning of our journey, I do not offer this book as a definitive end to getting the most out of life. There are other topics, other approaches to the subjects found here, and more wisdom to be shared by others who have experienced much more in life. Trying to create the ideal life from knowing all the right moves and words to use, however, is like attempting to create a flow chart for every situation you will be in some day. It will not be possible. Those moments will arrive when the answers are not revealed in a self-help book, a dynamic speech, or even the wisdom of a close friend. Like a meal without dessert, something will be lacking. To that end, may I share with you a way to maintain your passion for life and all its challenges, even when there seems to be no quick answers or easy solutions.

Before those moments arrive, may I suggest that you find someone who does have the wisdom to sustain you even in those moments of depression or frustration that no human words can ever help. Someone who understands our deepest desires and goals in life. A person who can give us the courage to go on even when the world tells us to stop. Yes, I am talking about God.

As I was writing this book, I knew that if it was to be an accurate reflection of my prescription for life, the book must include my faith in God. I wanted desperately at times to include it in various chapters (actually all of them) because I could hear your mental voice saying, "But what if that does not work, Jones?" It was tempting to put at the end of the section, "If all else fails, go find God's instruction… that's what I try to do." Doing so, however, would have been selfish on my part because I would have been taking advantage of a captive audience. Whacking people over the head with religion has never been my style. Rarely can one person force another to believe in anything. Instead, I prefer to plant small faith seeds (like saying "I am blessed" or referring to a higher power when talking with a group, or simply saying "God Bless You" at the end of a keynote) and hope people will talk with me afterwards about the meaning behind the words. One of the most rewarding parts of my current career has been the opportunity to talk with people about the motivation behind the motivation.

Being a practical thinker who prefers to-do lists over theory and flow charts over think tanks, it would seem contradictory to my nature to believe in something so many people find abstract. Nothing could be further from the truth in my life. Instead of always fretting over choosing this course of action or which words to use, I relate my situation to God through prayer and know He will give me the wisdom to make the decisions necessary for the moment. Please note that I did not say the right decisions, for my own selfish desires sometimes get in the way of hearing Him clearly. Even if I do make the wrong choice, having a relationship with God assures me that He will be there to comfort me regardless of the outcome... something we cannot say about most of the other relationships in our lives.

As a source for making my life prime rib, I am reminded of the phrase, "Life is God's gift to us. What we do with that life is our gift to Him." When someone gives us a special gift, our first inclination is to return the favor with an even bigger gift if possible to show our gratitude. Since God does not need a bread-maker or Teflon-coated pancake griddle, the only way for me to personally show my gratitude for what He has done for me is to live my life in concert with Him, reflecting Him in all I do. I fall short many times, but I keep striving to do my best. With that goal in mind, everything I do becomes an opportunity to be more like prime rib. Whether it is in restoring a strained relationship, spending time with my family, or making the most of my financial resources, God has some definite ideas for me to use.

Take the first chapter in this book, for example. Adding to the questions about how to use your abilities, what would change if the question, "What would God have you to do?" were put in place. With that question answered through prayer, circumstances, and the wisdom of other godly people, the way becomes a little clearer. The path you choose may not be easy, but you have the comfort of knowing that the Creator of the universe is on your team. I would take that over any learned skill or earthly self-help information any day.

Adversity (kites chapter) is another example. As we search for direction on escaping our current dilemma, what better person to enlist in our support group than the One who has seen it all? Even money management has divine implications. Before making a large expenditure, a sincere prayer for guidance or direction from God's Word can have a dramatic impact on the path chosen.

With all these examples, you may be thinking, "It sounds like you are saying that God should be instilled in every fiber of our being." Well…you're right. To truly be prime rib, God has to be a significant part of our life. It is His wisdom and comfort that must imbibe every part of our life if we are to know inner peace, another quality of prime rib people. Things may be falling down all around us, but our faith in God should be sufficient to sustain us in those times of turmoil.

Where to start

Having trudged through a myriad of lists in this book, you are no doubt expecting one to surface here. I am happy to oblige, but don't expect this list to be quite like the other ones introduced in our time together.

1) Travel about eighteen inches. In the average human body, the distance between the head and the heart is eighteen inches. It seems like a short distance, but you would be amazed at the number of people who have never made the mental journey. All their lives they have made decisions with their minds, only to find that doing so has not produced the results they had "in mind." Suppressing the tugging of their heart has created the feeling of an intellectual dead end.

If this sounds familiar, then try allowing those gentle nudges from your heart to be a factor in the decisions you make. God has given all of us a conscience, and yielding to it can help open the door not only to better decisions but to knowing God on a more personal level.

2) Talk with Godly people. Understanding how God works in their lives will not create a direct road map to knowing God, but it *will* offer a recipe of ingredients to use in creating your own fulfilling relationship with Him.

3) Pray. Even if you have never prayed before, give it a try. God does not want floury words or intellectual thoughts. He only wants you to share your innermost joys and sorrows with Him. Just tell Him what you are thinking and let Him do the rest.

Thanks for dining with me

There are a million other things I would love to share with you about this subject and many others, but that will be another book in the future. Maybe it will be a conversation we have after a conference or workshop. Whatever the mode, I do sincerely hope that your life is prime rib. In your quest for the best in all areas of your life, I also trust that you will include God as your host and allow him to determine your choice of entrees when the world offers so many choices. Adding that dimension to the strategies shared in this book may not always make things easy, but when you look back at your life at any moment, you can smile and take great pride in knowing that it was made up of the best things in life... that it is definitely prime rib.

Now slide back from the table and get busy. Someone out there is suffering from too much potted meat in their life and may need to dine with you.

*We all have our "potted meat" moments. This last page was ours. Sorry for the inconvenience!   **Jones**

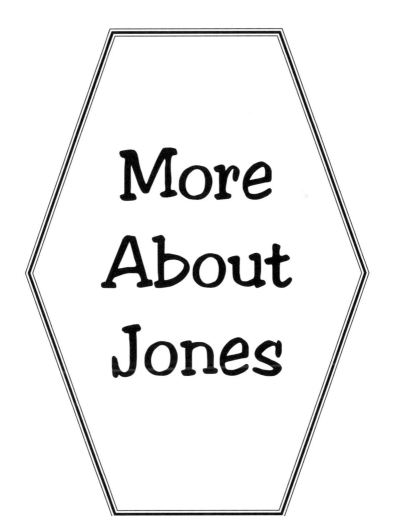

More
About
Jones

Jones Loflin

The Speaker With Two Last Names

When asked about the common thread in all his programs, Jones responds with "We should all be passionate about certain things in life, including our family, spiritual beliefs, career and relationships." A former classroom teacher, Jones travels throughout the United States, challenging and inspiring audiences young and old to live a life of excellence instead of mediocrity. Using strange props, eccentric singing, humor and a unique conversational style, Jones quickly captures the attention of groups ranging from elementary students to educators to parents, business groups and associations.

Jones' customized keynote addresses and workshops have made him a frequent trainer of organization officers and association leaders. His seminars are best described as entertaining, engaging and practical. Some of his most requested programs are:

Are You Packed For Success?
Why Build A Birdhouse?
Prime Rib or Potted Meat...The Choice is Yours!
From The Inside Out
Time Management and You

For information on booking Jones for your next conference or activity, contact:

H.O.P.E. Inc.
118 East Lawyers Road
Monroe, NC 28110
(704) 753-4811 (800) 853-4676
Fax: (704) 753-4809
jhope@perigee.net

To receive additional copies of

PRIME RIB OR POTTED MEAT?,

video or cassette tapes, contact:

H.O.P.E. Inc.

(704) 753-4811

(800) 853-4676

Quantity Discounts Are Available.